# The Cato Institute

The Cato Institute is named for the libertarian pamphlets *Cato's Letters,* which were inspired by the Roman Stoic Cato the Younger. Written by John Trenchard and Thomas Gordon, *Cato's Letters* were widely read in the American colonies in the early eighteenth century and played a major role in laying the philosophical foundation for the revolution that followed.

The erosion of civil and economic liberties in the modern world has occurred in concert with a widening array of social problems. These disturbing developments have resulted from a major failure to examine social problems in terms of the fundamental principles of human dignity, economic welfare, and justice.

The Cato Institute aims to broaden public policy debate by sponsoring programs designed to assist both the scholar and the concerned layperson in analyzing questions of political economy.

The programs of the Cato Institute include the sponsorship and publication of basic research in social philosophy and public policy; publication of major journals on the scholarship of liberty and commentary on political affairs; production of debate forums for radio; and organization of an extensive program of symposia, seminars, and conferences.

CATO INSTITUTE
747 Front Street
San Francisco, California 94111

# The Theory of Collective Bargaining 1930–1975

# The Theory of Collective Bargaining 1930–1975

## W. H. Hutt

**With a Foreword by Charles W. Baird**

CATO PAPER No. 14

INSTITUTE
San Francisco, California

*Rededicated to*
*Arnold and Edith Plant*

**Library of Congress Cataloging in Publication Data**

Hutt, William Harold, 1899–
    The theory of collective bargaining, 1930–1975.

    (Cato paper ; no. 14)
    Reprint of the 1975 ed. published by Institute of Economic Affairs, London.
    Includes bibliographical references.
    1. Collective bargaining.   2. Trade-unions.
3. Labor economics.   I. Title.
HD6483.H8   1980   331.89'01   80-36792
ISBN 0-932790-20-8

Printed in the United States of America.

CATO INSTITUTE
747 Front Street
San Francisco, California 94111

# CONTENTS

# FOREWORD

Few ideas are so deeply engrained in the minds of most people in the Western world as that labor unions have been beneficial to those whose main incomes derive from the sale of labor services. Labor unions are popularly credited with all, or most, of the improvements in real wages and working conditions that workers have enjoyed in the last 100 years. Labor unions, together with "enlightened social legislation," have been credited with converting capitalism from an economic system that served primarily the interests of the owners of physical and financial (nonhuman) capital into a more humane system that serves the interests of workers as well. Today's labor unions are thought by most people to be the culmination of labor's "long and bitter struggle" to get its fair share of the economic pie. Because of labor unions, it is asserted, it is no longer true that owners of capital get more than their fair share.

In *The Theory of Collective Bargaining*, W. H. Hutt explains why these common beliefs about labor unions are wrong. In order to fully understand Hutt's arguments, it is necessary to understand some basic principles of the operation of a voluntary exchange economy. In such an economic system the demand for any particular good arises out of the production of noncompeting goods. In order to demand effectively something you want to have, you must have something to offer for it in exchange. The way most people get the wherewithal to purchase the things they want to acquire is by allowing productive resources they own (labor time, capital, natural resources, etc.) to be used in the production of other goods and services in exchange for payments called incomes (wages and salaries, interest, rents, etc.). The flow of incomes arising out of production constitutes purchasing power over what is produced. The source of purchasing power over a product is the incomes-flow originating from the production of other goods. *Production* is the source of all demands. (Hutt fully develops this point in his 1974 book, *A Rehabilitation of Say's Law.*)

People who organize production (entrepreneurs) contract with suppliers (owners) of labor time, capital, and natural resources in order to be able to produce goods and services the entrepreneurs think other people want to acquire. The owners of the productive resources are willing to sell the services of those resources to entrepreneurs because they plan to use the incomes they receive to buy what they want to buy. An entrepreneur is willing to assemble productive resources and oversee their use in production because of the income he receives from doing so. The entrepreneur's income is a residual claim—what is left over out of gross receipts after all contractual claims are met. The residual claims of entrepreneurs, like the contractual claims of resource owners, are part of the total flow of incomes arising out of production.

The maximum price that an entrepreneur is willing to pay for the use of a resource is based on the physical productivity of the resource and what his customers are willing and able to pay for the product or service he is producing. The minimum price that a resource owner is willing to accept in any specific hiring contract depends on the values the resource owner attaches to alternative uses of the resource. The more attractive and numerous the alternative employments of the resource available to its owner, the higher will be the minimum price its owner will insist on getting as a condition for allowing his resource to be used by any particular entrepreneur. In other words, the more attractive and numerous the alternative employments, the better the bargaining power of the resource owner vis-à-vis any individual entrepreneur. Competition determines what prices will actually be observed in hiring contracts. Given the number of workers who can do a particular kind of job, the larger the number of entrepreneurs who are actively seeking the services of such workers, the closer will wages be to the maximum prices the entrepreneurs are willing to pay. Similarly, given the number of entrepreneurs actively seeking to acquire the services of a particular type of worker, the larger the number of workers who can and offer to do the job, the closer will wages be to the minimum prices workers are willing to accept.

The most common reason given for the belief that unions benefit workers is the notion that an individual worker necessarily has weaker bargaining power than an individual employer. Unions, it is thought, rectify that imbalance. Hutt begins the present study with a thorough examination of this bit of conventional wisdom. He shows that although some famous economists, including even Adam Smith, made some remarks to the effect that workers individually have weak bargaining power, none of them ever satisfactorily explained why that should be. Hutt claims that Adam Smith implicitly gave up the idea as his analysis developed. Hutt also shows that collusions among employers not to compete for labor, far from being a source of labor's weak bargaining power, were responses to earlier combinations of workers that put individual employers at a disadvantage.

As we saw above, bargaining power depends on alternatives. Since substantial real economic growth has taken place over the last 100 years, those who rest their case for the efficacy of unions on labor's supposed weak bargaining power must, in order to be consistent, conclude that the usefulness of labor unions approached zero many years ago. The best friend workers have had in terms of their bargaining power is the automobile. The automobile greatly increased the mobility of labor and thereby increased the number of employment alternatives effectively available to workers of all types. Workers owe more to Henry Ford than to Samuel Gompers and George Meany combined.

Hutt argues that gains to labor in hiring contracts can only come about by the expansion of the flow of incomes that originate out of production. Since what entrepreneurs are willing to pay workers depends on what their customers are willing and able to pay for what is produced, it is to the advantage of workers that those customers have lots of purchasing power. Since real purchasing power comes only from incomes earned in the production of real goods and services, it is to the advantage of workers that real productive activity expand. Moreover, increased real productive activity, by making available more and diverse employment opportunities for each worker, increases the bargaining power of workers.

The sine qua non of labor unions is the strike—the collective withholding of labor services in particular employments together with the prevention of other workers' serving as replacements. Since such withholdings diminish the flow of incomes (referred to by Hutt as the "wages-flow") from production, they must act to the detriment of workers as a whole. A few individual workers may be made better off by such withholdings, but workers as a group cannot benefit. (In his 1973 book, *The Strike-Threat System,* Hutt surveys many empirical studies of the effects of unions and shows that in fact labor union activity has not benefited workers as a whole.)

The only way a labor union can keep a wage in employment $A$ higher than the wage paid to workers with similar abilities in other employments is to block access to employment $A$. Union shop and closed shop contracts as well as violence and threats of violence are favorite devices used to do so. Apart from the coercive character of such activities, they are to be deplored, according to Hutt, because they further diminish the incomes-flow upon which the welfare of workers as a whole ultimately rests. The incomes-flow is maximized when labor is efficiently allocated among alternative employments. If, given the quantity of workers in employment $A$ and the demand for product $A$, the wage paid in $A$ exceeds that paid to workers with similar abilities elsewhere, that means that the value people place on additional units of product $A$ is higher than the value they attach to what would have to be given up in order to have more of $A$ produced. The lower wages paid in the alternative employments are based on what buyers of these alternative products are willing to pay for them—i.e., the value buyers place on them. If a union did not block additional workers from entering employment $A$, some workers would transfer, increasing the supply of labor (relative to its demand) in $A$ and decreasing the supply of labor (relative to its demand) in the alternative employments. Wages would fall in $A$ and rise elsewhere until the discrepancy disappeared. More of product $A$ and less of other products would be produced; but since the values previously placed on additional $A$ exceed the values previously placed on the sacrificed units of the alternative products, the total flow of incomes would increase.

Hutt emphasizes that the *threat* of a strike does more harm to workers than actual strikes. The productivity of workers, which, as we saw earlier, affects what entrepreneurs are willing to pay for labor time, depends to a large extent on the quality and quantity of tools and machines the workers get to use. Unions are better able to appropriate some of the returns that ordinarily would accrue to capital owners when capital equipment is already set up in very specific forms. When a firm using types of machines and tools that cannot be converted to other employments is unionized, it is highly probable that the owners of the capital will lose some income. Since the capital is already set up and cannot be converted to alternative uses, its owners will have little bargaining power vis-à-vis the union. Any individual's bargaining power, whether the person is a seller of labor time or a seller of capital services, depends on the person's alternative employment opportunities. Because of the strike threat, suppliers of capital services will be reluctant to acquire specific capital goods. They will hold their capital in nonspecific forms in order to protect themselves. This distortion of the types of capital made available for workers to use in production implies lower productivity and less efficiency than otherwise would exist. The incomes-flow, and therefore the welfare of workers as a whole, is thereby impaired.

Of course, the damage done by the threat of strike is difficult to measure empirically. We know a priori that the strike threat will adversely affect the production of capital goods, and we can measure the incomes-flow that accompanies that production; but there is no way to measure what the incomes-flow would have been with an undistorted array of capital goods. Because this cost of labor union activity is invisible, it is usually ignored in discussions of the effects of labor unions.

The bottom line of Hutt's analysis is that any gains made by members of any particular labor union relative to what they would have received without the labor union must come primarily at the expense of other workers and consumers—not owners of capital and entrepreneurs. Far from being the instruments of social justice that they are routinely considered to be, labor unions (however legal) are merely conspiracies in restraint of trade that make most people poorer than they would be otherwise.

The first edition of *The Theory of Collective Bargaining,* written in 1930, included only parts 1 and 2 of the present essay. Part 3 was added in 1975 to demonstrate that the original thesis had been corroborated by the experience of forty-five years and to clarify and amplify its exposition. The resulting package is an effective attack on the mythology of private sector labor unions.

Membership in private sector labor unions as a percentage of the labor force has been declining in the United States in the last ten years. Currently public employee unions are the only unions experiencing significant growth. The common belief that unions were necessary for private sector workers to get their fair share explains much of the attractiveness of public sector unions to government employees. Hutt points out in chapter 4 of part 3 that it is silly to try to construct a defense of public employee unions along the same lines usually used to justify private sector unions. After all, how many people would be willing to take seriously the charge that public employees are exploited "by avaricious, undertaxed taxpayers." But even more fundamentally, since, as Hutt argues, unions have not been beneficial to private sector workers, much of the appeal of public employee unions is based on a false premise. I hope the reprinting of this significant work will lead to a wider appreciation of that fact.

April 1980                                                    Charles W. Baird
                                                              Hayward, California

# AUTHOR'S PREFACE
## to the Second Edition (1975)

Over the forty-five years since this book was first published, further reading and thought on the topic have confirmed the broad, simple conclusions that I reached in 1930. But as my understanding of the issues has deepened, I have come to perceive that the harm caused—especially to the lower-income groups—by the imposition of labor costs by coercion is even worse than I originally perceived in the 1930s. Not only is the aggregate real value of output considerably reduced thereby, but the regressive incidence of the burdens is, I can now show, more than I had then realized.

Part 3 of the present (second) edition analyzes the grounds for these assertions. It deals also with questions that had not arisen when the first edition was published in 1930 and, above all, with the responsibility of "wage-push" for inflation (or rather for the *political expediency* of inflation). Parts 1 and 2 remain unchanged, and expressed in pre-Keynesian language.

The reader will find many references to my 1973 book, *The Strike-Threat System,* which treats in more detail many of the issues briefly touched upon in part 3, and answers numerous predictable objections. Two other contributions of mine are relevant to the developments I now discuss. *Politically Impossible...?,* 1971, is directly relevant to the prospects of reform, and *A Rehabilitation of Say's Law,* 1974, attempts to explain rigorously why downward wage-rate adjustments in recession tend to induce increased employment of labor. Such adjustments are most powerfully "stimulative," I argue, not in the occupations in which they occur, but in noncompeting activities.

The other major improvement (as I regard it) of my new exposition lies in the emphasis I now place on the *composition* of the assets stock and the composition of the stock of complementary assimilated knowledge and skills (in reaction to prospective strike-threat depredations: part 3, chapter 4). I now maintain as fundamental that the harm caused by *fear* of strikes is even more damaging to society than that caused by strikes themselves.

My interest in the consequences of the "collective bargaining" process dates back to 1925, when Edwin Cannan asked me to write a paper for his economics seminar on the effects of union pressures upon income distribution. The paper suggested, with due deference to the then accepted theory, that they could exert no *general* redistributive power. Continuing to think about the consequences, I reached the tentative conclusion that tolerance of the private use of coercive power via the right to strike was the crucial factor in the British malaise of the 1920s. Yet public opinion, I observed, condoned strikes solely through the illusion that their use, or threatened use, for defense or aggression, could achieve a redistribution of income from rich to poor, or somehow rectify labor's supposed "disadvantage in bargaining." Not a single economist I could then trace seemed to have stated in print what I had come to feel economists ought to be teaching.[1] That is why I came gradually to feel that I should write this book.

When the first edition appeared, I was naive enough to expect that it would have at least some early influence. I was soon disillusioned. I sent copies to several persons prominent in the British trade union movement, including the Webbs, for whom I then had the highest respect (pp. 1, 8). Only W. A. Appleton, secretary of the General Federation of Trade Unions, responded; he was appreciative. But the *International Labour Review* refrained from mentioning it, although its argument was almost a direct challenge to the original purpose of the In-

---

[1] Böhm-Bawerk's *Control or Economic Law,* which reached very similar conclusions, had not been translated into English, and I was unaware of it. The German edition was published in December 1914, after its author's death. The English translation appeared in 1931. It is now available in *The Shorter Classics of Eugen Böhm-Bawerk,* (South Holland, Ill.: Libertarian Press, 1962).

ternational Labour Office, of which the *Review* was the official organ.

I dedicated the 1930 edition of this book to Arnold and Edith Plant. They had been my closest friends and companions during the years 1928–29 at the University of Cape Town, while Arnold had been a candid and kindly critic. In unfading gratitude I rededicate the present book to them.

Since I write in the United States I should add that part 3 applies to the United Kingdom and Western societies generally.

*University of Dallas, Texas*
*April 1975*                                    W. H. HUTT

# I. Labor's "Disadvantage"

The object of this essay is to controvert the suggestions typical of most modern economic textbooks, (a) that there is some portion of the normal remuneration of labor which, in the absence of collective bargaining by labor is, or can be, transferred to the remuneration of other factors of production owing to labor's "disadvantage in bargaining"; or (b) that combination, by increasing labor's "bargaining power," enables it to acquire a part of the normal remuneration of some other factor.

*The term "collective bargaining"*

The very useful term "collective bargaining" was coined in 1891 by Mrs. Sidney Webb in her work on the cooperative movement. The Webbs[1] have never given a formal definition but have used it to cover negotiations between employers and workpeople when the workpeople act in concert and the employer meets "a collective will." Collective bargaining may take place in many kinds of negotiating in concert, but it is used here to describe what is probably the most important function of trade unionism.

*The supposed importance of the abandonment of the Wage-Fund Theory*

It is commonly believed that the overthrow of the "Wage-Fund" theory was the turning point in regard to the

---

[1]This is the only sensible way of referring to Lord Passfield and Mrs. Webb. No disrespect is intended. It is the penalty of their greatness.

economist's attitude towards trade unionism. The earlier economists, we are told, held that the level of wages depended on the proportion of the wage fund or capital in relation to the number of workers. Trade unions could not affect the size of this fund and hence all efforts to raise the general level of wages were futile. Gains by one section of the workers could only be obtained at the expense of other sections.

With the abandonment of the wage-fund error, however, and especially after John Stuart Mill's renunciation of it in 1869, this view was shown to be untenable, so we are told, and from that time the economic justification of trade unions has been complete. Professor Henry Clay, for instance, tells us that the wage-fund theory was responsible for the belief, common in the middle class, that political economy had found trade unionism to be futile because of the theory that

> if wages were fixed by the proportion between population and capital, trade unionism was futile and wicked; it could raise the wages of one section only at the expense of other sections.[2]

Successive reiterations by leading economists have caused this belief to become firmly accepted. F. A. Walker, in 1876, declared that under the wage-fund doctrine the striking workman was regarded as "an irrational animal whose instincts, unfortunately, were not politico-economical."[3] F. Y. Edgeworth, writing in 1881, declared that

> in the matter of trade unionism...the untutored mind of the workman had gone more straight to the point than economic intelligence misled by a bad method.[4]

Cunningham, in 1892, said:

> Men were continually regretting the blind stupidity of working men who thought that combinations could raise wages...but this was a blunder. Combinations can raise wages; they have done so and may do so again.[5]

This belief in a fundamental change having been effected by giving up the clumsy wage-fund theory is erroneous and

---

[2]*Economics for the General Reader*, p. 313.
[3]*The Wages Question*, p. 144.
[4]*Mathematical Psychics*, p. 45.
[5]*Economic Journal*, 1892, p. 14.

misleading. The realization of the absurdities of the doctrine gave the apologists of the unions something they could attack with the full support of authority; but the productivity theory which, in various forms, arose on its ruins did not in itself contain any justification for collective bargaining. The vague phrases about the "disadvantage" of uncombined labor which constitute its modern defense have existed continuously since the days of Adam Smith.

*Attempts to rationalize ideas about "Labor's Disadvantage"*

The change of doctrine that was supposed to have taken place in the 1870s was heralded by four mainly independent[6] but remarkably similar defenses of workers' combinations. The authors were: F. D. Longe, Cliffe Leslie, Fleeming Jenkin, and W. T. Thornton. Three of them definitely attacked the wage-fund conception, but the principal object of all four, although Longe denied it, was the justification of unionism.

These contributions all appeared during the years 1866 to 1869, and were followed in 1869 by an article from Mill (in the *Fortnightly Review*), who, it seems, had only read the views of his friend Thornton. It was in this article that he formally renounced the wage-fund theory and gave *currency* to the view that there was some way in which trade unions could gain, not at the expense of other workers but at the expense of the capitalist. An attempt to analyze separately and carefully every single theory put forward by all these writers has led to the conclusion that they consist largely in the rationalization of ideas about labor's disadvantage in bargaining which, far from being novel, had been held continuously since the time of Adam Smith. For the rest they seem at first to contain little beyond a number of attacks on the general theory of prices based on generalizations induced from the consideration of a number of hypothetical and improbable special cases, and a number of newly coined descriptive phrases which have since served as a substitute for thought in these matters.

*The idea of "Labor's Disadvantage" accepted by*
*wage-fund theorists*

Adam Smith, who was the first to talk about "the funds destined for the payment of labor," held views about the laborer's disadvantage which were not unlike those of Marshall. McCulloch had a typical defense of workers' combinations. It is only when workers act, he said,

> in that simultaneous manner which is equivalent to a combination...that it becomes the immediate interest of the masters to comply with their demand.
> [Without] an open or avowed, or [of] a tacit and real combination, workmen would not be able to obtain a rise of wages by their own exertion, but would be left to depend on the competition of their masters.[7]

Even Fawcett, the wage-fund die-hard who, for many years after Mill, his master, had given up the theory still clung affectionately to it, held quite the usual sort of views justifying collective bargaining. "I believe it can be easily shown," he wrote,

> that the laborer is placed at a disadvantage, if he attempts simply as an individual to arrange this bargain, and I further believe that labourers must show that they have the power of combining, in order at all times to be able to sell their labour on the best possible terms.[8]

The ultimate defense of unionism in Mill's 1869 article—the bold justification of monopoly—differed in no respect from the justification which he put forward in his *Principles* whilst he still believed in the wage fund. Those excluded did not suffer for their wages would, in any case, have been kept down to subsistence level. "Combinations to keep up wages," he wrote, "are therefore not only permissible, but useful, whenever really calculated to have that effect."[9] On the other hand, the chief critic of the supposed new tendencies, T. S. Cree, in an essay praised but not heeded by Marshall, declared that "the correctness of the wages fund is not at all necessary for my position."[10] Curiously enough, the two authorities whose condemnation of unionism was almost unconditional objected also to the wage-fund conception. Mountifort Longfield's *Lectures on Political Economy,* 1834, is notable chiefly for its anticipa-

---

[6]Leslie *had* read Longe, some articles by Thornton and Jenkin, and Jacob Waley's paper (referred to later).

[7]*Treatise on Wages,* p. 79.

[8]*Economic Position of the British Labourer,* 1865, p. 173.

[9]*Principles,* chap. 10.

[10]*Criticism of the Theory of Trade Unionism,* 1891, p. 24.

tion of the productivity theory; yet its object was, to use his own words, "to show how impossible it is to regulate wages generally either by combinations of workmen, or by legislative enactments." And Hermann in Germany blamed the wage-fund error for encouraging unionism and causing strikes "by its doctrine that the source of wages is the capital of the 'entrepreneur'...."[11]

These facts seem to have been overlooked by the Webbs or else regarded by them as of no importance at all. For, in seventeen references to McCulloch and three to Fawcett in their *Industrial Democracy,* they make no mention of the grounds on which these economists sought to justify unionism; and they are two of the three authorities quoted in a footnote (on page 606) to support the contention that belief in the wage-fund theory as enunciated by them was the reason why public opinion "unhesitatingly refuted Trade Unionism."[12] In twenty-five references to Mill they do not quote the grounds on which he approved of their monopolistic policy. Neither do they notice the arguments of Mountifort Longfield, whose name appears in a footnote. And they quote a passage suggesting the wage-fund formula from Cree, but do not mention his claim that the theory was irrelevant to his criticisms.

Articulate trade-union leaders accepted readily the wage-fund formula. At least two sets of trade-union rules actually quoted McCulloch,[13] thousands of whose pamphlets circulated among and were approved of by working-class leaders of his day.[14] An essay which declared the orthodox political economy of the 1850s to be undisputed[15] was passed by a large union as a faithful representation of their views.[16] Even the supposed enemies of unions had often absorbed the typical belief in their

[11]Quoted by Crook, *German Wage Theories,* p. 28.

[12]In an earlier draft of part of this essay, circulated to a number of friends, I wrongly included C. Morrison as a wage-fund economist accepting the doctrine of "labour's disadvantage."—W. H. H.

[13]E.g., "Articles of the West Riding Fancy Union...1824," quoted in *Report of the Select Committee on the Combination Laws,* 1825, p. 27. Cf. a *London Trades Committee* report in 1838 (p. 5), in the Place Add. MSS. 27835: 104.

[14]E.g., Place Add. MSS. 27803: 294, 347, 478, 516.

[15]T. J. Dunning, *Trade Unions and Strikes,* 1859, pp. 4–5.

[16]A recent writer puts the date of the change in the attitude of unionism in the 1890s. Hitherto,"...it had taken for granted the current doctrines of 'the

beneficence. Sheriff Alison, detested by the unions for his stern suppression of the disorders of the famous Glasgow cotton spinners' strike of 1838, gave evidence (before the Parliamentary Enquiry on Combinations, 1838)[17] to the effect that workmen's combinations enabled the "members to a certain degree to compensate and to enter with equality into the lists with capital," and by 1860, as Sir Archibald Alison, his views had not changed. "Without combinations," he said, "competition would force wages down and workers would be reduced to the condition of serfs in Russia or the Ryots of Hindostan."[18]

### The theory of collective bargaining a mere attachment to whatever wage theory has been held

The truth is, that the theory explaining or showing the desirability of collective bargaining has always been quite independent of the wages doctrine that has existed at any time; it has been very similar in form no matter to what particular theory it has been attached; but it has always been a kind of attachment to the theory and not, as we should expect, in view of unionism being the most obvious institution forming part of the wage-determining mechanism, an integral part of it. This fact alone would suggest that nothing very important or fundamental is involved in such a theory.

A few economists have ignored it altogether in a way which would suggest that they regard it as empty although they have not directly attacked it.[19] For example, Professor Cannan writes:

> Modern doctrine teaches plainly enough that combinations of earners can only raise earnings if they can raise the value or quantity of the product....[20]

This clearly cuts out any theory of collective bargaining, for that is concerned with the *distribution* and not the *size* or *value*

---

wages fund,' 'the law of supply and demand' and so forth." (Rayner, *The Story of Trade Unionism,* p. 63.)

[17]Q. 1956.

[18]*Rep. of the Nat. Assn. for the Prom. of Social Science,* 1860.

[19]The recent publication of Cannan's *Review of Economic Theory* provides an exception to this statement.

[20]*Theories of Production and Distribution,* 3rd ed., p. 404.

of the product. He adds that in practice it is shown by common observation and careful investigation that little can be done by combinations of earners unless they have power to prevent outsiders from entering the trade.[21] All that is admitted here is that individual groups may gain at the expense of others by monopoly obtained by the device of exclusion; and that was what the earlier economists appeared, at times, to say.

But *does* direct exclusion supply a sufficient explanation of the effect of combinations on wages? It is desirable briefly to examine this view before discussing the theories which appear to contradict it.

*The interests of the unionists are antagonistic to those of the laboring masses*

Frederic Harrison described the trade-union movement as "one universal protest against injustice from the whole field of labour." This identification with the general working-class movement (although very common) may be highly misleading. It probably arose from the fact that typical ignorant upper-class opinion during the nineteenth century was quite unable to appreciate the complexity of the social and economic tendencies operating among the "lower orders." To them, there was only one working class—an inferior class that, led by demagogues and agitators, was trying to usurp political and economic power. Apart from the economists, a few enlightened industrialists and a few philosophers, they had a vague belief that the drudgery of the masses was necessary for the leisure of the few, that their subservience was the natural order of things, and that low wages were good for trade. They were very glad to have it on the authority of the economists that these evil and rebellious combinations were ineffectual.

But this should not allow the modern student to ignore the fact that the interests of the unionists were almost universally antagonistic to those of the laboring masses. Had historians of the trade-union movement been orthodox economic theorists, they might have laid the strongest emphasis on this point. As it happens, however, they have been practically without excep-

[21] Ibid.

tion persons with an undisguised hostility to orthodox theory; and this may account for their failure to stress what might have struck other economists most forcibly. The Webbs frankly admit the frequent existence of monopolistic tendencies on the part of unions, but the general impression they leave is misleading for they have obviously written as union advocates. However much we may admire their *History*—a monumental achievement which it would be presumptuous to praise—we must remind ourselves, whilst we are influenced by its thoroughness and manifest sincerity, that it is yet the special pleading of those who have devoted their lives to the encouragement of the institution whose development they were recording.

### Opinions of working-class leaders

To justify the contention that combinations were antagonistic to the interests of the great majority of the laboring classes is impossible by means of ordinary historical method in a mainly theoretical treatment such as this. We can, however, to escape the suspicion of bias or misrepresentation, appeal to the opinions, expressed at different times, of working-class leaders themselves. This is not the most satisfactory way of indicating the position, but it is the most practicable one in the present case.

### The "founder of scientific socialism"

We might appeal first to William Thompson. Described by Menger as "the most eminent founder of modern scientific socialism," the originator of the idea of "surplus value,"[22] a friend and teacher of Robert Owen, Thompson can hardly be regarded as a biased witness against working-class bodies. He was, we are told, of the most kindly and gentle disposition, but when he considered the workmen's combinations of his day he was moved to passionate condemnation of them. To him they were "bloody aristocracies of industry."

> The apprenticeship or excluding system [he said] depended on mere force and would not allow other workers to come into the market at any price.

[22]According to Menger. It has been disputed by Dr. Bonar among others.

> It matters not [he said in 1827] whether that force...be the gift of law or whether it be assumed by the tradesmen in spite of the law: it is equally mere force.[23]

They demonstrated to him

> the inefficiency of force-supported regulations, though backed with political power, to keep up generally throughout the country the remuneration of any species of labour; though they certainly have tended...to keep up the remuneration of the few within the circle of the combination.

Such gains were always

> at the expense of the equal right of the industrious to acquire skill and to exchange their labour where and how they may.[24]

This is "the founder of scientific socialism" speaking—not an employer.

> Will they then resort to force, law supported as to apprenticeships or illegal as to intimidation—in all cases equally hateful—to put down the competition of the great majority of the industrious and thus erect a bloody—for force will lead to blood and without blood no aristocracy can be supported—aristocracy of industry?[25]

### *A South African parallel*

The position which raised the ire of Thompson a century ago finds a close and obvious parallel in South Africa today. If he had been writing at the present day, and the South African trade unions had condescended to reply, they would probably have answered: "Those whom we exclude are, on the whole, 'non-Europeans,' a morally inferior class to whom we do no harm by our exclusive policy as, owing to their low standard of life, they cannot rise and can merely drag us down." Curiously enough this was just the view of the English unions of last century towards the "knobsticks" or "scabs," the great majority of the laboring classes who were outside the unions. Their typical attitude was well summarized by J. S. Mill in his attempted justification of enlightened unionism in 1869. *Acting*

[23]*Labour Rewarded,* 1827, p. 75.
[24]Ibid., pp. 76–7.
[25]Ibid., p. 81.

*as the unions' advocate* he put the following words into the mouth of their witness:

> Those whom we exclude are a morally inferior class of labourers to us; their labour is worthless and their want of prudence and self-restraint makes them more active in adding to the population. We do them no wrong by intrenching ourselves behind a barrier, to exclude those whose competition would bring down our wages, without more than momentarily raising theirs, but only adding to the total numbers in existence.[26]

*Apart from the Malthusian aspect,* this argument seems to be a fair representation of trade-union opinion at the time Mill wrote.

## The apathy of depressed classes

One may wonder why it was that the working classes in England did not protest more at such injustices. To some extent it may have been for the same reason that we get so few protests against unions from "non-Europeans" in South Africa. It often appeared as if the "knobstick" felt and believed himself to be an inferior person. Another friend and defender of the trade-union movement, writing a year before Mill in the passage just quoted, described the knobstick's position thus:

> The wretched knobstick...is jeered at and snubbed on all possible occasions...he receives none of those little aids by which the other men lighten one another's labour...he is generally an inferior workman, and his work receives its full due of criticism; he is an outcast, a pariah, and fear of personal violence is not required to render this position a wretched one. Some societies will not allow him to work in the same shop with their members, even as though he tainted the air...Odd as it may seem, the knobstick takes much the same view of his position; he feels himself a sneak....He is unskilful, poor, weak and a traitor (for attempting to undercut); they are skilled, rich, strong and noble; yes, even when they morally kick him...[27]

## Protests against exclusiveness

Mill's attempts to justify exclusiveness did not pass without criticism. "After all," said Dr. Stirling,

[26]*Fortnightly Review,* 1869.

[27]Fleeming Jenkin, "Trade Unions," in *North British Review,* 1868, reprinted in his *Collected Papers.* Compare Webb, *History,* p. 296.

the knobstick is not an outlaw, to be cut off from personal freedom and the protection of the law. He has his rights like his betters; and though too often treated like the leper of old, his chief offence is, after all, his poverty.[28]

And T. S. Cree, referring to the Malthusian backing to Mill's argument, remarked that Malthus "never proposed the destruction of the weak by the strong, in order that the latter should have more to divide."[29]

### Unionist apathy to Chartism

Until they obtained political power the great mass of the laboring classes had few friends outside their own ranks. Apart from the fact that there were no classes below them whom they could exploit by exclusion, they could not afford the luxury of unions or any other societies; nor could they pay leaders. Organizations of laborers offered no careers to competent organizers until well on into the nineteenth century when the course of economic progress had greatly increased their resources. Thus we find that the Chartist Movement, the most prominent genuine working-class movement of the earlier half of the century, received little support from the unions. Their apathy brought fierce denunciation from Feargus O'Connor. "Never," he wrote, "was there more criminal apathy." The denunciations of Daniel O'Connell went much deeper. He condemned in the severest language not only the existing practices of the Irish unions but also the essential exclusiveness of all attempts at the regulation of wages by combination.[30] The reply of the London Trades Combination Committee to O'Connell was hardly repentant.[31]

### In more recent times the old antagonisms still occasionally apparent

When at length, owing to the growth in the economic and political power of the masses, unionism began to extend its ranks, the hostility to the older interests was obvious. John

[28]Stirling, "Mr Mill on Trades Unions," in *Recess Studies,* 1870, p. 330.
[29]Cree, *Criticism,* p. 28.
[30]Cf. Ryan, *The Irish Labour Movement, pp. 89, 90.*
[31]*Combinations Defended,* 1839, p. 42.

Burns, in the 1890s, was contemptuous of existing unions. "Mere middle and upper class rate-reducing institutions," he called them. The "Dockers' Strike" which he organized heralded a new era which brought into trade unions workers in unskilled occupations. This led to a rapid expansion during the late 1890s and the early part of this century, during which period the earlier tendency to hostility tended, for many reasons, to die down. Not that the opposition of interest had gone. In the 1890s exclusiveness still had its unashamed apostles. Miss Clementina Black admitted that no doubt trade unions did "tend to make the battle of life harder for the incompetent and shiftless." They tended, she said,

> to make a boundary line on the one side of which is the well-paid man in work and the other side the absolutely unpaid man out of work.

But this, she argued, brought no real injury to the community.[32]

### The "New Unionism" obscured but did not destroy the old opposition of interest between one class of workers and another

Nevertheless, as the proportion of organized workers grew the real antagonism between those with effective exclusive power and those without became more and more obscured. Some regarded the "New Unionism" as a movement which completely superseded the old and exclusive system.

> "The Masses" have been as ready to group themselves in exclusive sections, according to income, as their "betters," [said H H Champion in 1890] and the greatest sinners in this respect have been the Trades Unionists. But of late a different feeling has arisen...[33]

Whether exclusive power or desire was checked in the nineties is doubtful: but it was certainly not becoming more noticeable. Occasionally, however, we still found an overearnest or disgruntled leader refusing to deny the existence of the old antagonisms. "The exclusiveness of some of the existing unions," said Tom Mann in 1911,

---

[32]*Contemporary Review,* 1892.
[33]*The Great Dock Strike,* 1890.

> must be got rid of. . . the skilled men must throw off that silly no-
> tion of superiority. . . That unionism whose object is to maintain
> a special preserve for the privileged few must disappear, for it is
> incompatible with the rights of workmen generally and is a
> menace to industrial solidarity.

In America we see the same thing. From the IWW we occasionally get the same kind of protests against exclusiveness.
And the French "syndicalists" have expressed themselves in
almost the same words.

### Excluded classes still apathetic

But from the classes who, in modern society, suffer most
from union exclusiveness we get the fewest protests. They accept quietly and unquestioningly their traditional economic in-
feriority. When the "coloured" or "native" workers in South
Africa organize, or when women organize in countries which
are racially homogeneous, we either find them establishing new
exclusions or else adopting the principle of "equal pay for
equal work"—thus renouncing the only means in their power
of discounting the prejudice against them as a class. Of course,
organization of such workers is sometimes necessary in order
to get or preserve the effective or even the *legal* right to a trade.

### The "Standard Rate" essentially an excluding device

The exclusive policy of unions is not confined to the obvious
method of visible exclusion by apprenticeship restrictions and
the like. Every insistence on an artificially high rate will tend to
reduce the number it will be profitable to employ. Those within
the combination will still benefit at the expense of those outside. This method of obtaining monopoly is more pernicious
than that of apprenticeship exclusion as it enables the
monopolists to plead that they are acting in the interests of
those whom they are in fact excluding. They can claim that
they are raising the standard of living of the very ones whose
competition they wish to eliminate, and even get the support of
legal enactment to enable them to carry out their policy. The
evil in labor monopolies lies not only in their driving the less
fortunate to relatively badly paid occupations but also in their
raising the cost of living to them as well.

*The wage-fund theory did not justify the popular belief that
political economy condemned all strikes as irrational*

In view of the obviously purely monopolistic nature of
workmen's combinations in their day, there is nothing surprising in the classical economists' failure to give much attention to
the question as to whether or not the members of a union could
increase their incomes otherwise than at the expense of other
workers. *An elaborate theory of collective bargaining would
not have been much more than the merest academic abstraction
in their day.*

Where they can be blamed is in not having faced more boldly
this question of exclusiveness. It is true that on the whole they
condemned it, but they seemed rather reluctant to admit its
power. They often appear to have been trying to leave the impression that all strikes must necessarily fail in the long run and
that no group of workers could gain permanently by strike action. This sort of thing was very comforting to the employers
and the press, and until the 1870s it was made use of in the
most careless manner. The economists were said to have
declared that combinations could not raise wages. If they were
right the workers were fools. But surely what the economists
(apart from their sophism about labor's disadvantage) had
been saying or trying to say was that unions could not raise
wages in general: it had never been explicitly denied that particular groups could, by combination, increase their own share
of the wage fund at the expense of others, although it was
sometimes argued that such monopolies were bound to break
down in the end through the competition of other workers
(generally from abroad), or through capital being driven
elsewhere.

The inadequacy of the wage-fund conception allowed this
careless thinking to persist—comforting employers yet having
no effect in preventing strikes. But modern theories would
credit unions with some power of benefiting their members
without the exercise of exclusiveness. Let us examine how the
various ideas contained in these modern theories came to be
held.

*The idea of "Labor's Disadvantage" is found
in* The Wealth of Nations

The distinctive ideas that lie behind still-persisting theories which seek, without defending monopoly, to justify collective bargaining, originated, as has already been pointed out, with Adam Smith. They arose in connection with the subsistence theory he put forward. Mr. C. M. Lloyd, a leading advocate and historian of unionism, either does not realize this or is very ungrateful for it.

> The influence of manufacturers [he writes] . . . bore heavily upon Parliament. . . in 1776, this influence was reinforced by Adam Smith's *Wealth of Nations,* from which it appeared that the creed of unrestricted exploitation was really a new gospel for humanity.[34]

This is a strange way of referring to one of whom it has been said: "[his] sympathies, indeed, seem to have been wholly with the industrious wage-earner, and especially with the poorest."[35] To suggest that Adam Smith favored low wages is entirely false. The suggestion is constantly reiterated that the classical economists generally "defended subsistence wages."

> Of all the libels upon them invented by socialist and semisocialist writers [says Professor Cannan] this is about the worst. They may have been, they certainly were, wrong about the causes of high wages, but they were always in favour of them.[36]

The real evil in the subsistence theory lay in its hopelessness, and the attitude of self-pity and dependence which it tended, right against the spirit of the age, to instill in the minds of the laboring classes. Harriett Martineau, whose views are so often misrepresented as harsh, was attacked by the *Edinburgh Review* for her sentimentalism. They wrote:

> From a wish, we suppose, to address the men in conciliatory language, she condoles with them as a suffering race who were included to strike by the depression of their wages to the lowest point.

### Adam Smith limited his theory to "ordinary occasions"

Adam Smith's views bearing on what became later the theory of collective bargaining arose then out of the subsistence

[34]C. M. Lloyd, *Trade Unionism,* p. 4.
[35]Cannan, *Economist's Protest,* p. 422.
[36]Ibid., p. 423.

theory. "Upon all ordinary occasions," he wrote, "the masters have the advantage in the dispute," and can force the men "into a compliance with their terms."

His explanation of this vague power can be analyzed into three separate ideas. First, there existed particular combinations of masters who agreed to force down wages to subsistence level. Second, there was "a tacit but uniform combination" among employers to keep wages down. Third, that although in the long run the workman might be "as necessary to his master as his master is to him," the necessity is "not so immediate." Whereas masters,

> though they did not employ a single workman, could generally live a year or two upon the stocks which they have already acquired, [many workmen] could not subsist a week, few could subsist a month, and scarce a year without employment.[37]

These factors, he thought, accounted for the employers' power to force wages down to the subsistence level. He seems to have assumed that *how* they gave the employers this remarkable power was self-evident, for no further explanation of them was given.

The emptiness of the theory becomes clear when we consider the limits he assigned to the employers' power in this respect. The limits were determined, not by the individual's minimum requirements for survival, but by those of his family, because otherwise, said Smith,

> it would be impossible for him to bring up a family, and the race of workmen could not last beyond the first generation.

But as Professor Cannan asks, if the masters have this power why should they concern themselves about the labor supply of the next generation? "Trade rings," he says, "usually adopt the motto, 'After us the deluge,' " and he points out that Adam Smith himself probably thought the doctrine was weak, as evidenced by his dragging in an irrelevant reference to such wages being the lowest "consistent with common humanity,"[38] Moreover, observing that in practice wages were often considerably higher than subsistence level, Smith limited the application of his theory to "ordinary occasions."

[37] *Wealth of Nations,* book 1, chap. 8.
[38] See Cannan, *Theories,* p. 235.

*Adam Smith himself seems to have unconsciously
given up the idea*

Do the *exceptional* occasions help us to understand the theory? He mentioned only one exceptional occasion, and that was an "increase of revenue or stock" which would "sometimes give the labourers an advantage, and enable them to raise their wages." They could do this because the masters would then "bid against one another in order to get workmen, and thus voluntarily break through the natural combination of masters not to raise wages." This, he thought, would happen whilst expansion was in progress. Thus we arrive at the really remarkable conclusion that an increase of stock *loses* the masters their relative advantage, a conclusion which could be made to look like a direct contradiction to the previous contention that it was the greater stocks held by the master which gave him his advantage. The truth is that Adam Smith had really unconsciously given up his earlier theory. In Professor Cannan's words:

> The power of the masters to depress wages to the subsistence level by combination, and their "common humanity" which prevents them killing the goose that laid the golden eggs, by depressing them below that level, both disappear....So little room is left for the subsistence theory that Adam Smith seems, towards the end of his work, to have forgotton that he had ever held it.[39]

But the ideas about the employer's advantage and his power to force down wages indefinitely and the workman's corresponding disadvantage which originated thus have persisted right through to the present day, although the basis on which Adam Smith himself had founded them had been tacitly renounced.

*Masters' combinations for dealing with wages
seem to have been reluctant and retaliatory
until late in the nineteenth century*

We shall now proceed to examine the history and development of the three ideas that were connected with his statement

[39] Ibid., p. 237.

of the subsistence theory. We shall deal first with the allegation that masters habitually formed themselves into combinations to force wages down. (The *power* of masters' combinations to force down wages will be discussed at a later stage.) Some informal combinations of masters undoubtedly occasionally got together in his day; and there is no reason for believing that these combinations were anything new. More's *Utopia* talks about a "conspiracy of rich men," discussing "how to hire and abuse the work and labour of the poor for as little money as may be."

This kind of idea probably recurred from time to time right up to the time of Adam Smith. Nevertheless, his contention is misleading. Workmen's combinations equally existed in his day, and it is a question of some importance whether masters' combinations led to the formation of unions or whether it worked the other way. A recent article by Mrs. Dorothy George has shown that the long-held belief that the Combination Laws were used in a grossly partial way against organizations of working-men is erroneous,[40] and it is the writer's impression that throughout the greater part of the nineteenth century the extent of combination of capitalists for the express purpose of settling wages was negligible.

Adam Smith's contention was repeated by J. B. Say, but it did not pass without criticism. It was categorically denied in 1834, by E. C. Tufnell, a very able observer with an almost unrivaled knowledge of English industrial and labor conditions:

> What may have been the case in the time of Adam Smith we have no means of ascertaining, but certainly for a long period back there is no reason to suppose such a state of things to have existed.[41]

Right through the century we find similar denials from trustworthy observers. The Committee on Artisans and Machinery of 1824 could find only one instance of a perfect combination of masters—twelve type founders.[42] It is difficult

[40]*Econ. Jour. History Supp.*, 1927, p. 214.

[41]*Character, Objects and Effects of Trade Unionism*, 1834, p. 99. Tufnell is criticizing the phrase about "tacit combination," but he undoubtedly had formal combinations in mind.

[42]A great deal of further evidence could be brought forward to support this

at times to know what observers understood by "masters' combination."[43] Certainly, however, deliberately organized bodies on the lines of the unions were almost nonexistent until late into the century. The early industrialists were imbued with a sturdy individualism that was repugnant to association. As Dr. Stirling pointed out:

> The oft-quoted dictum of Adam Smith, that it is easy for a few capitalists to combine, is a grievous error... [they are] necessarily competitors, and therefore kept apart by natural rivalries.[44]

"A combination of rival traders," said Buchanan, "is a phenomenon which, until human nature is changed, will never be exhibited." [45]

> The same principle of selfishness which prompts them to form the league, prompts them also to break it.... Rival traders have no confidence in each other; no two of them will ever act in concert.[46]

A similar attitude was taken by McCulloch and others.

### Employers combined to counter "the strike in detail"

Until the 1880s this attitude was, to a superficial observer at any rate, correct. The aversion of employers to enter even into protective or defensive associations was brought out in evidence before the Trade Union Commission of 1867. That evidence suggested that the motive of employers' associations—reluctantly entered into—was self-defense. Very early in their history, combined workers had discovered the utility, as a coercive weapon, of the device so aptly named by the Webbs, "the strike in detail." Practically all the combinations among employers that were revealed by the inquiries in 1824 or 1825 were either retaliatory against unions exploiting "the strike in

---

point, but an adequate analysis of it would necessitate lengthy treatment. (The Select Committee on Artisans and Machinery, 1824; the Select Committee on the Combination Laws of 1825; and the Place Collection contain a large store of evidence on the point.)

[43] There is no suggestion, of course, that the accounts of capitalist combination in the eighteenth and nineteenth centuries in Levy's *Monopolies, Trusts and Cartells* and other works are in any way misleading.

[44] Stirling, *Trade Unionism,* reprint from second edition (1869), 1889, p. 40.

[45] Buchanan's editorial note to the *Wealth of Nations,* vol. 1, p. 210.

[46] Editorial note ibid., vol. 1, pp. 206–7.

detail'' or else the employers' side of ''joint monopolies'' operating with the encouragement and connivance of the workers. We shall discuss the latter later on.

A good example of ''the strike in detail'' occurred immediately after the repeal of the Combination Laws, when the Linen Weavers of Barnsley planned to compel workers, factory by factory, to strike, selecting the order by lot. The object was to coerce employers one by one, thus enabling the strikers to be supported out of contributions from those still working for other employers. The *Edinburgh Review,* commenting on this device in 1838, said that those who adopted it were generally victorious, and that this caused them to acquire the habit of considering themselves irresistible. ''They produce,'' said the *Review,* ''a universal conviction of the necessity of a combined resistance.'' Tufnell gave a description of the reluctant formation of a masters' association at Leeds following a strike in detail.[47] Many trustworthy observers gave this reason for such employers' combinations as then existed. In the middle of the century we find the same opinion held. W. L. Sargant, a student with an intimate knowledge of working-class movements, wrote in 1851:

> I have shown that combinations among the men are inevitable, and where the workmen combine, masters will and must do the same.[48]

In 1854 Morrison expressed a similar opinion and described the forms that employers' counter combinations could take.[49] In the late 1860s even trade-union advocates spoke of masters' associations as though they were *novelties.*

> In the last dispute in the iron trade, [said Longe] employers taught an unruly and high-paid class of workmen the wholesome lesson that employers can combine as well as labourers.[50]

Thornton, in a passage largely contradictory of other parts of his work, wrote:

---

[47]Tufnell, *Character,* pp. 101–2.
[48]*Science of Social Opulence,* p. 404.
[49]*On the Relations of Labour and Capital,* 1854, pp. 98–99.
[50]*Refutation of the Wages Fund Theory.*

> Hitherto want of concert between individual masters has placed
> them at a great disadvantage as compared with the men...The
> lock-out is never initiative—it is always retaliatory.[51]

Another friend of the unionists was sufficiently naive to attribute inconsistency to employers *who during a strike* had entered into a combination "such as they did not hesitate to stigmatise in those who were not so well educated as themselves."[52] And the cry of an employer of about the same time has a sincere ring.

> As yet war has only been declared on one side....As yet capital
> has been passive, but it will not remain so long; it must soon, in
> self-defence, combine to defeat the tyranny of labour, and who
> then can doubt the result?[53]

The studies of Mr. W. Page for the period 1886 to 1890 seem to have suggested to him the same ephemeral and retaliatory character of employers' combinations. He states quite simply:

> The combination for bargaining purposes of all classes of
> workers necessarily resulted in a like movement among the
> employers.[54]

Contemporary observers of the rapidly developing trade-union movement in the British Dominions in the early 1890s tell the same story. Referring to a great strike which had just failed owing to the employers getting together, a writer from Australia said that it proved that,

> difficult as it was for employers to risk their rival interests
> against a common enemy, they will do so and receive public support
> in the most democratic countries, so long as labour makes a
> demand which the public holds to be arbitrary or unfair.[55]

A New Zealand observer about the same time, writing on "Labour Troubles in New Zealand," declared that, apart from a shipowners' association,

> no other combination of employers was formed in this country
> until after the strike commenced. The natural conclusion is that

[51]*On Labour,* 2nd ed., 1870. p. 271.

[52]Samuelson, *Friendly Hints to Trade Unionists,* 1867.

[53]*Capital and Labour,* 1867, by a member of the Manchester Chamber of Commerce.

[54]*Commerce and Industry,* p. 333.

[55]H. H. Champion, in *The Nineteenth Century,* February 1891.

the aggression of labour forced employers to combine in self-defence.[56]

## *The question is of less significance in modern times*

This rapid historical survey is based on a more or less arbitrary selection of opinions expressed by competent observers at different times during the last century. But again and again the writer has found evidence of the extreme reluctance with which competing interests have agreed to cooperate in their own defense and of the ephemeral nature of any associations which have thereby resulted. Since the late 1880s other causes have led to the aggregation of capital on such a large scale that an inquiry as to whether employers' associations are primarily bodies which take initiative in labor questions or merely retaliatory, loses its significance.

## *Joint support by opposed combinations*

The motive for these combinations of masters was probably something more than mere direct defense, the opposing of the coercive device of "the strike" by that of the "lockout." We have early evidence of workmen's societies being countenanced by the masters and used as instruments against factories which were "underselling." And we find unions claiming that their sole object was "to protect the upright manufacturer against the unfair competition of the avaricious one, and to secure a fair remuneration for labour."[57] But this very important phenomenon can be best discussed at a later stage.

## *"Tacit combination" by masters*

Let us turn now to the rather vaguer but frequently quoted suggestion of Adam Smith's, that the employers were everywhere in a tacit but uniform combination to keep wages down. This has probably been more frequently quoted because, in its vagueness, it is more difficult to refute. It is quite understandable that in the time of Adam Smith masters

[56]*Econ. Jour.,* 1891, p. 716.
[57]John Wade, *History of the Middle and Working Classes,* 1833, p. 284.

had a kind of conception of the wages of a laborer as something definite, fixed, and natural. Wages then varied slowly, and any master would naturally resent having to pay more than he had been accustomed to; but this would not prevent wages from rising. If there had been a tendency for wages to rise, it is quite certain that masters would have compared notes on meeting one another and complained of the iniquity of it. They would have done all in their power to avoid paying more; but the point is, could they have succeeded in keeping wages stationary? Pepys recorded how he paid his first maid three pounds a year and her clothes. A new cook who came later demanded four pounds, and he wrote: "...the first time I ever did give so much." Later still he wrote:

> Wages are very considerable; a fat Welsh girl who has just come out of the country, scarce understood a word of English, capable of nothing but washing, scouring and sweeping the rooms...[received] six guineas a year, besides a guinea for her tea (*Pepys's Diary*).

And Defoe in 1725 deplored the fact that

> women servants are now so scarce that...their wages are of late increased to six, seven, nay eight pounds per annum and upwards.... But the greatest abuse of all is that these creatures are become their own lawgivers; they hire themselves to you by their own will. That is, a month's wages or a month's warning (*Everybody's Business, Nobody's Business*).

However, the indignation and disgust of these gentlemen did not enable them to escape paying the higher wages caused by the scarcity; and we have no reason to suppose that they acted any differently from other masters of their day. It was the very futility of such "tacit combinations" which led to the seventeenth-century attempts to get the justices to force maids into service and to assess their wages.[58]

The same thing applies to the alleged tacit combination on the part of the farmers. The typical farmer is still notoriously stupid over the matter of wages—constantly complaining of the shortage of labor, and when asked why he does not offer higher wages, indignantly replying that laborers ought to be only too grateful to get work at the wage he is offering. But this

---

[58]E.g., Brown, Bland, and Tawney, *Select Documents,* pp. 360, 361.

spirit does not lower the price of labor: it simply results in the farmer's demand being somewhat less than it might otherwise be, for the shortage of which he complains remains. If he prefers that "shortage" to raising wages, presumably the existing rate is the economic one. Ultimately, all the dictum about a tacit combination comes to is that masters will not pay more than they believe to be necessary to get the labor they desire; and this does not operate solely on the employers' side. Laborers similarly will not offer to work for less than they believe they can get: the "Clay-Martin" Report of the South African Economic and Wage Commission, 1925, alleges a tacit combination on the part of natives not to accept less than a certain rate of wages. This merely means that they know what they can get; the phrase simply sums up a typical attitude of mind, an attitude which may perhaps help to maintain stability or may act as an unavailing resistance to necessary change.[59]

### The masters' necessities "not so immediate"

If the "tacit combination" theory exercised much influence because of its vagueness, still more does this seem to be the case with the third idea which we have seen sprang from the *Wealth of Nations*. To Adam Smith the masters had the advantage because their necessity for the men was "not so immediate" as that of the men for them, for whilst the master could subsist for a long time upon stocks acquired, many men "could not exist for a week, few could subsist a month, and scarce any a year without employment." Although writing in the eighteenth century, he put it much more mildly than many modern writers, who talk as though any unemployed worker is faced with immediate starvation. We must remember, however, that this idea was held by Smith as a sort of appurtenance to and amplification of his subsistence theory which, as has already been shown, was quite erroneous and, moreover, apparently given up by himself.

The theory was kept alive in a general way by the Socialists, whose "exploitation theory" may have been the source from

---

[59]There is no suggestion, of course, that the psychological phenomenon of a group of competitors tacitly endeavoring "not to spoil" a buying or selling market (in a time of change) does not exist.

which the idea was so strongly reinforced in the late 1860s. Said Louis Blanc:

> Who so blind as not to see that, under its domination [competition], the continuous fall of wages, far from being exceptional, is necessarily universal.

Many of the economists who condemned the exploitation theory put forward, nevertheless, the rather milder theory of "the employers' advantage"; and it appears as if they were not uninfluenced by it. The theory of the employers' advantage causes the worker, as one writer put it, to visualize the capitalist as a "Gulliver of labour, only to be mastered by the united efforts of Lilliputian numbers."[60] It is surprising that the idea obtained such a wide acceptance. Appeal to facts could have given little support to it. "Nine-tenths of the cotton-workers," said Tufnell, criticizing the theory, "never think of forming Unions, and the alleged advantage has never been taken of them."[61] Said another writer:

> To tell a "baffled contractor" wanting to get labour that "nothing but a close combination" can give workers "even a chance of successfully contending with employers must sound in his ears like dismal mockery.[62]

And in the words of yet another critic:

> The labourer...is at no disadvantage in bargaining with the employer, who is tied to his machines, which he must keep fully employed, or perish financially.[63]

In the writings of Thornton and the other authors of the late 1860s mentioned above, attempts to justify or rationalize the theory took various forms, only some of which it is worth while examining. As has been suggested, these attempts appear to be little more than inventions of vague phrases, which, if conveying a clear meaning to some economists, have served as mere catchwords and substitutes for thinking by others.

---

[60]Stirling, "Mr. Mill on Trades Unions," in *Recess Studies,* 1870, p. 317.
[61]*Character,* p. 96.
[62]Stirling, "Mr. Mill on Trades Unions," p. 319.
[63]Cree, *Criticism,* p. 20.

### *"On terms of equality"*

One of the most common is that combination puts the worker "on terms of equality" or "on an equal footing" with the employer; it gives him "equality of bargaining strength."[64] Can we give any definite meaning to this term "equality"? Thornton tried to. He took an example of a product created by the joint contributions of one worker and one employer and assumed that if they were on "an equal footing" the product would be divided equally between them. This is so absurd that one wonders that he ever allowed it to get into print, but it gave him an opportunity of himself criticizing the vague phrases used by others. He thought that he had dealt with it satisfactorily merely by contradicting it. And he added:

> Nothing is easier than to show that if labourers were really on the same footing as their employers, the equality between them would after all be but a sham and a cloak for the extremest inequality.[65]

### *The worker "has no reserve"*

The idea is made a little more explicit when it is developed into the theory that the worker is at a disadvantage because he has no reserve. The derivation from Adam Smith is obvious. The capitalist "has the advantage of past accumulations in striking his bargain," runs the formula; he can "discharge a single workman with comparatively slight inconvenience, while the workman loses the whole means of subsistence."[66] The employer, it is held,

> can generally wait longer for labour than labourers can wait for wages....This is why the price of labour is generally so much depressed.[67]

### *Exaggerations and confusions introduced by these ideas*

Without the subsistence theory to rest upon, such conceptions appear to be the emptiest of sophisms. Sometimes

---

[64]The use of the terms "strong" and "weak" in economic literature was criticized by Pantaleoni in the *Economic Journal,* 1898, p. 193.

[65]Thornton, *On Labour,* p. 192.

[66]"Committee on Trade Societies of the Nat. Assn. for the Prom. of Soc. Sci.," in *Transactions,* 1860.

[67]Thornton, *On Labour,* p. 175.

Smith's moderate dictum about the relative urgencies of the master's and workman's necessities is exaggerated into the statement that the latter must take whatever the employer offers or starve. Thornton, trying to justify this view, was led into the wildest exaggerations. He contended first that the individual laborer could not "carry his labour to a better market or spare the time to go elsewhere," a contention that the slightest examination of the labor mobility of his day would have upset; and to this argument he added, that savings would avail him little.[68] Possibly, he had noticed that workers with savings were getting no more wages for the same work than those without, but with this admission what becomes of the "labourer has no reserve" theory? We are forced to the conclusion that there is some distinction between collective saving by the union and individual saving, or that individual reserve funds are no reserves at all. If this is the case, Thornton's attempted expansion and generalization of the particular theory also falls to the ground.

> Price [he said] in any particular instance will be greater or less according as it is the buyer or seller who is best in a position to take advantage of the other's necessities.[69]

But the only explicit meaning given for "necessities" is lack of a reserve, so that if savings "avail little" the whole idea is meaningless.

If the argument had been that poverty acted as a restriction on the mobility of the laborer, and so prevented him from selling his services in the most profitable market, it would have appeared more plausible. There is a suspicion of this idea in the passage just quoted, but it is confused with the "reserve fund" idea, and suggests that the disadvantage arising from lack of mobility can be overcome without restoring mobility. Surely the plain truth is that we can make no useful generalizations on this matter at all. It might be argued with equal justification that the worker without savings has an advantage over the worker with savings because he has nothing to lose.

[68]Ibid., p. 102.
[69]Ibid., p. 143.

*The "dependence" and "insecurity" of the worker*

Most writers who use these ideas are less explicit than Thornton, and so less easy to criticize. With some, the worker's disadvantage seems to be implicit in the relationship of "employer and employed" (as it is called), and the alleged "dependence" of the worker resulting therefrom. The phrase "employer and employed" is in itself greatly misleading, for the ultimate employers of labor are the consumers, and it is on their demand that the workers are dependent.[70] The development of this relationship did not bring, however, any obvious new disadvantages. On the contrary, the *security* of the working class was greatly increased. The *Edinburgh Review* in 1837 could speak about "the comparatively perfect security of the working classes in later times"; and Nicholson could point out, towards the end of the century, that

> the wage-earners of this country as a whole. . . have a much more
> stable income than the mass of peasant proprietors in other
> countries; the yield to labour on the large system of industry is
> much more *certain* than the yield to land of the *petite culture*.[71]

There is no reason for supposing that the relationship of the wage earner to society is less stable than that of the poor proprietor.

*Contradiction of these ideas by "the pin money" argument*

It is enlightening to oppose to these arguments another one, curiously enough often naively used by the same writers, which completely contradicts them. It argues that the possession of a reserve, or the relative *absence* of necessities (i.e., a lower conventional standard of life), far from causing higher wages to come to the possessor, leads to lower wages. In one of its forms it is sometimes called "the pin money" argument. The contention is that those who have some other source of income or some alternative income can, on this account, have their wages forced down. In another of its forms it might be called "the standard of living theory of wages." The suggestion is that a certain body of workers (usually alien immigrants or nonwhite

[70]Cannan, *Review of Economic Theory,* pp. 433–43.
[71]*Econ. Jour.,* 1892, p. 482.

residents among European peoples), on account of their being accustomed to a lower standard of living, find themselves earning lower wages. They get less, it is said, because they have fewer requirements. According to the particular sentiment attaching to the people concerned, we are either told that they are "exploited" or that they are themselves the evil party in persisting in undercutting. But the economics of the phenomenon are wholly explicable in terms of the effect of the characteristics of the workers upon their supply.

## Labor sold "without reserve"

Thornton put forward also a rather different form of the conception of the laborer's lack of a reserve. He declared that the price of labor was determined on different principles from that of other commodities because it was "sold without reserve." "Isolated labour," he said, "is almost always sold without reserve, whereas tangible commodities are scarcely ever so sold." How is it that high prices are secured? "Plainly, by not selling unreservedly." That is true enough if it merely means that some part of the supply is held back; but as will be seen when we come to the form of the theory which says that "labor is perishable," the phrase is probably based on fallacious reasoning. Even Mill, who showered extravagant praise on Thornton's book, pointed out that "reserving a price is, to all intents and purposes, withdrawing supply."[72] The most careful analysis does not reveal that it means anything more than that uncombined labor cannot exploit monopoly power. Quite often this is clearly all that is meant when it is said that the workers are "at the employers' mercy." For example, the executive of an American trade union declares that if skilled work could be obtained without the necessity of years of experience,

> any craft would be thrown open to the competition of an almost unlimited labour supply; and the craftsmen in it would be practically at the mercy of the employer.[73]

[72]*Fortnightly Review,* 1869.
[73]Quoted in L. C. Marshall, *Industrial Society,* p. 562.

## Labor is "a perishable commodity"

Another form taken by the idea that labor is exploited because it cannot wait is that which says that labor is a perishable commodity. We have to thank or blame Thornton for this form of the idea. "Labour," he said, "...will not *keep*." Criticism soon came.[74] Even General Walker, who believed that in his final overthrow of the wage-fund theory he had provided a justification of trade unionism, attacked the idea. His criticism was not altogether satisfactory. It was based partly upon a hairsplitting point about time spent in rest not resulting in waste, but in labor being "stored up,"[75] and partly upon a contention that the buyer of labor was in precisely the same position.[76] "If he does not buy to-day's labour to-day," wrote Walker, "he surely cannot buy it to-morrow"; and he went on to say that with a cessation of industry the employer would become "industrially defunct" when he had eaten up his capital, whereas the laborer in "preserving his thews and sinews preserved also his stock in trade and his industrial ability." A criticism by Nicholson in 1892 went nearer to the point:

> A man who cannot employ his capital loses his income as surely as a labourer out of work loses his wages.... If the one is perishable, so is the other. We are constantly reminded that a labourer is liable to dismissal, and thus indirectly to starvation and death. But though this may be true of a labourer it is not true of labour. To say that all the labour of a country, or even a considerable part, could be dismissed by capital, is palpably absurd.[77]

By all odds the best criticism came from Pierson:

> Thorton's argument is defective. The "keeping" of labour—supposing it could be kept—would not diminish the supply of labour; it would simply delay it. At a given moment there would be fewer people offering to sell their labour; but their number would be all the greater later on. Organisation in a particular trade is capable of achieving its purposes, because, in a particular trade, it is capable of permanently limiting the supply

[74]J. E. Cairnes criticized the theory privately to Thornton.
[75]*The Wages Question,* 1876, p. 292.
[76]Ibid., p. 294.
[77]*Econ. Jour.,* 1892, p. 480.

of labour. But this limitation leads to an increase in the supply of labour in other trades; and if all workpeople were organised, the conditions under which alone a Trade Union can exercise a permanent influence upon the rate of wages would nowhere be fulfilled.[78]

One would have thought, after such criticism as Pierson's, that the phrase "labor will not keep" would have disappeared for ever from the economic textbooks; but it cheerfully persists. Marshall continued to explain that labor was at a disadvantage in bargaining because it was "perishable."[79] Probably through his influence the idea has become sanctified in current economic jargon;[80] thousands of students have repeated it parrotwise in examinations; and when Mr. R. G. Hawtrey in 1926 ornaments the idea with flowers and epigram we do not feel shocked.

> What he withholds to-day, [says Mr. Hawtrey] cannot be sold to-morrow, for labour is more perishable than cut flowers. To-morrow, to-day's labour will no longer exist.[81]

He does not merely mean that if the laborer (from his own fault or owing to the defects of economic organizations) does not work, the time he has wasted cannot be regained. He holds that, because the worker cannot acquire an accumulated stock of his labor and defer selling when the market seems to require it, "he is only too likely to sell his services at a price below that which the market, properly approached, might yield him."[82]

[78]Pierson, *Principles,* vol. 1, p. 270.

[79]Marshall, *Principles,* 3rd ed., p. 647.

[80]The extent of the hold which this idea possesses is seen in the erroneous attributing of the phrase: that "a strike fund would make labour less perishable, and therefore, as far as bargaining strength was concerned, more on a par with capital," to a workman in 1831. (Economic History Supplement of the *Economic Journal,* no. 3, p. 388.) The passage in the *Cambrian* (October 1, 1831) on which the above words are based reads as follows: "...that if they had been associated with the clubs in time past, they might have opposed a reduction in wages and obtained relief if the attempts to reduce [wages] had been persisted in."

[81]Hawtrey, *The Economic Problem,* p. 29.

[82]Mr. Hawtrey's discussion involves a point about the worker's disadvantage in not being "a specialist in the art of selling," and the phrase "properly approached" may have had the whole of this idea in mind. In essence, however, the argument appears to be the same as that which Pierson criticized.

*The survival of the "subsistence theory"*

The persistence of all these theories seems to be in part due to the survival of the subsistence theory superstition, the idea that wages tend "naturally" or through competition to fall to "the lowest point" or "a minimum," although as we have seen, Adam Smith gave no logical explanation for the belief, but merely assumed that because wages could not be below that level they could not be above. Thornton and Mill, we have seen, were influenced by it. Even Walker was led by a similar kind of belief to justify unionism. He argued first that *imperfect competition,* which operated against the worker, might lead to a disadvantageous bargain in the first place and that the low wage resulting would become perpetuated through consequent inefficiency. In such circumstances, he said, there was no "tendency in any economical forces to repair the mischief." After an illustration of how this worked, he brought in a theory of a different kind. Not only was there no tendency in purely economic forces to right the evil, but they themselves tended to perpetuate it. "Such disasters aside," he said (referring to his illustration),

> the tendency of purely economical forces is continually to aggravate the disadvantages from which any person or class may suffer.... Every gain which one party makes at the expense of another, provides the thews and sinews of war for further aggressions.[83]

Yet, like other economists, Walker probably had misgivings on this subject, as evidenced by his reversing the *apparent* original meaning of the passage last quoted, in the otherwise identical passage in his *Political Economy,* published later. He inserted the words: "under impaired competition," which considerably weakened the suggestion that purely economic forces tend to perpetuate rather than to counteract the results of originally disadvantageous bargains.[84]

---

[83] *The Wages Question,* pp. 165–66.

[84] The revised passage reads: "Irrespective of anything catastrophic, the tendency of purely economic forces, under impaired competition, is continually to aggravate the disadvantages, etc." (*Political Economy,* 3rd ed., p. 265.)

## Low wages and inefficiency

Outside the ranks of the more orthodox economists we find a host of prolific writers who have blamed competition itself, rather than its impairment, for "the tendency of wages to a minimum." The idea probably found its crudest expression in the writings of Charles Kingsley and the Christian Socialists, and undoubtedly exercised a great deal of influence through the antisweating movements. It has received lengthy and deliberate treatment in the Webbs's *Industrial Democracy,* and is one of the main bases of their advocacy of unionism. Marshall's treatment of the idea certainly did not give authority to the view that "economic forces" or competition tended to depress the worker, but it was similar to Walker's in holding that the disadvantageous position of the worker was cumulative.

> It lowers his wages, [he wrote] and as we have seen, this lowers his efficiency as a worker, and thereby lowers the normal value of his labour.[85]

This amounts to saying that there is a dynamic force tending to cause wages to fall through the decreased efficiency of labor.

Views of this sort are popular, but are usually accepted very uncritically. Economists have always noticed that where the standard of living is low there is low efficiency; and there is no doubt that a low standard of living is often an important factor causing that low efficiency; but this does not in itself allow that there is a dynamic tendency downwards. Surely this generalization puts the cart before the horse. In so far as low wages are due to inefficiency, from whatever cause, the right thing to do is to tackle that inefficiency directly. Interference with the price mechanism seems to be the very worst way of trying to deal with it.

There is, however, no theoretical solution to this particular question—it must be answered by appeal to experience; and yet, if there were anything in the idea, would not employers have discovered it? Few of them are unaware of the effect on efficiency of the stimulus of piecework, of making increased

[85]Marshall, *Principles,* 3rd ed., p. 649.

income the certain reward of improved efficiency. May not their general doubt that increased reward will automatically bring greater efficiency be due to the simple fact that in general it does not?

# II. Indeterminateness
## of the Price of Labor

*The early groping towards the idea of indeterminateness*

In the late 1860s what appears to have been an entirely new idea was brought into the discussion of collective bargaining. It seems to consist in the rationalization of an idea which had for long vaguely existed in "the untutored mind of the workman," but which previous economists, according to Edgeworth, had wrongly condemned as fallacious. The workman knew that if he argued and haggled with a shopkeeper about the price of an article he might obtain it for less than its marked price; and on this analogy, he did not see why, by threatening to strike, he should not obtain more wages for his labor.

This theme was borrowed by the economists and developed by them into a theory that the price of labor was indeterminate, and that within the range of its indeterminateness trade unionism had a legitimate field of action, in the same way that there was a valid field for haggling in the indeterminateness of barter. It was towards this notion that Thornton, Jenkin, Longe, and Leslie were in fact confusedly groping—towards a conception of the indeterminateness that exists under conditions that we now call "bilateral monopoly." Their groping was very blind, for competition on both sides (not monopoly) was generally blamed for labor's disadvantageous bargain.

*Formerly, the indefiniteness of isolated bargains seems to have been thought unimportant*

The earlier economists appeared to assume, either tacitly or expressly, that the indefiniteness of any particular bargain was of no importance. They were merely concerned with market

35

price, which they regarded as both the resultant of the in-
numerable individual bargains and the index of the level to
which all prices would tend, and from which, in the presence of
competition, they could not greatly diverge. Longfield, for instance, started with the case of barter, but did not think it
worth while analyzing, as "In all civilised societies goods are
exchanged for money or sold." Moreover, whilst he recognized
quite clearly the opposition of interest which led every individual "to buy as cheap and to sell as dear" as he could, he
did not go to the trouble of pointing out the possible ratios of
exchange which could arise in any individual case, because in
practice we have "the law of mutual competition."[1] Some
degree of freedom of competition he seemed to take as ax-
iomatic.

> As this state of freedom nearly exists in all civilised countries, [he
> wrote (after a reference to the forces in the labour market)] the
> principle just mentioned is not to be considered as a hypothetical
> axiom, but both it and the consequences drawn from it are truths
> of considerable importance.[2]

In a hypothetical isolated case, he knew that the results of a
bargain between two people would be *indeterminate,* although
he did not use this word; but the ratio resulting from that
theoretical example had no relation to any rate that would be
established in practice.

> A labourer working for himself [he wrote] would find it to his in-
> terest to give 19/20ths of the produce of his labour to the person
> who would lend him [a spade], if the alternative was that he
> should turn up the earth with his naked hands.

But this rate is not paid because of the competition of capital
for employment and because the profits of the least-paid
capital "regulate the profits of the rest."[3]

A writer in a later age might have expressed the same thought
more clearly, perhaps, by saying that, whatever the "curve of
indifference" of the laborer might be, he would not have to
pay more than the market price for the use of capital. Neither

---

[1] *Lectures on Political Economy,* 1834, p. 46.
[2] Ibid., p. 67.
[3] Ibid., p. 195.

profits nor wages, he thought, were determined by the "intensity of demand," which is "the sacrifice we would make to obtain any commodity, if the alternative were to be compelled to remain without it."[4] Longfield has been quoted at length because he was here deliberately setting on one side as unimportant, ideas which were later thought to be novel, revolutionary, and fundamental. And his judgment seems to have been right.

### The evolution of the idea

The first clear statement of the "indeterminateness" idea the writer has found in English economic literature is in a paper read to the Royal Statistical Society in 1867 by one Jacob Waley. He argued that the sharing of the gross return of industry between capital and labor would be "in a perpetual flux and never have time to settle into a state of stable equilibrium...." He continued:

> I conceive that there will in general be a large margin of uncertainty as to the division of the returns, and that the precise place at which the line is drawn will to a very considerable extent be determined by circumstances which may fairly be called fortuitous, and may be greatly influenced by a bargain between the employer and the employed.

In such a case it was quite possible that a strike would be successful. This is as clear and as moderate a statement of the theory as is to be found anywhere. There are passages in F. D. Longe's essay which suggest that he had the idea in mind, and Fleeming Jenkin in 1868 had some conception of it. (We cannot here discuss the several interesting fallacies in Jenkin's able work.) He said that the division of the produce between capital and labor was "purely a question of bargain"; and it could legitimately vary "within very wide limits."[5]

In 1869 Thornton helped to spread the idea by a violent yet vague attack on supply and demand generally (*On Labour*, 1869).[6] At times, when reading his book, one imagines that he

---

[4]Ibid., p. 194.

[5]Fleeming Jenkin, *Collected Papers*, p. 22.

[6]At first published as articles, then incorporated in *On Labour*, 1869 (two editions).

must have regarded the price mechanism as a completely arbitrary affair; but the work is so full of apparent contradictions that one can never be sure of his real meaning. (I am giving so much attention to Thornton because of the extent of his influence on this topic and because his contribution received extravagant praise from Mill.) His contention was that

> the price, whether of labour or anything else, in no case whatsoever depends upon the proportion between supply and demand.[7]...The propositions of supply and demand do not hold good under ordinary circumstances.[8]

For supply and demand he substituted "competition," which would suggest a mere verbal quibble; but he asked: "What regulates competition?" (p. 79) and replied:

> Nothing. There is no regularity about competition—competition is not regulated at all...there is no law of competition (p. 80).

We cannot follow him into the arguments which led him to this strange conclusion, but the notion seems to have arisen out of his expansion of a few special and for the most part quite unlikely cases into generalizations. This is so despite his claim to have covered nearly the whole field of possible cases with his examples. Mill did not fail to see this point; he admitted that most of the examples were, "on the face of them, altogether exceptional,"[9] but it was out of a criticism of some of Thornton's illustrations that he developed his theory of indeterminateness.

### The probable first use of the word "indeterminateness"

One of Thornton's arguments was illustrated by an auction; and he showed how the price at which a particular article would actually exchange hands might be different according to whether bidding was up or down. Mill pointed out that to establish the point of this example he had to suppose

> the case to be an exception to the rule that demand increases with cheapness: and since this rule, though general, is not absolutely universal he is scientifically right...but...in the general market

---

[7]Ibid., 2nd ed., p. 44.
[8]Ibid., p. 49.
[9]*Fortnightly Review*, 1869—reprinted in *Essays and Dissertations*, vol. 4.

of the world—it is the next thing to impossible that more of the commodity should not be asked for at every reduction of the price.

In spite of this severe criticism he admitted that Thornton had

> proved that the law of supply and demand is not the whole theory of the particular case...what he has shown is that the law is, in this particular case, consistent with two different prices, and is equally and completely filled by either of them. The demand and supply are equal at 20s. and equal also at 18s. The conclusion is not that the law is false...the phenomenon cannot help obeying it, but there is some amount of indeterminateness in its operation, a certain limited extent of variation is possible within the bounds of the law....

This is probably the first use of the word "indeterminateness" in this sense.[10]

## Cases which the supply and demand doctrine of price "does not reach"

Mill then went on seriously to discuss some of Thornton's other examples, to show that the laws of supply and demand still stood. He gravely pointed out, for instance, that in one case

> at £50 there is a demand for twice or three times the supply; at £50 0s.0¼d. there is no demand at all. When the scale of demand is broken by so extraordinary a jump the law fails of its application....

And in another case he remarked:

> Here, again, the author is obliged to suppose that the whole body of customers (24 in number) place the extreme limit of what they are prepared to pay rather than go without the article exactly at the same point...the case is just possible in a very small market—practically impossible in the great market of the community.

Nevertheless, from these examples Mill reached the conclusion:

> when the equation of demand and supply leaves the price in part indeterminate, because there is more than one price which would fulfil the law, neither buyers nor sellers are under the action of any motives derived from supply and demand to give way to one another.

[10]Thornton had used the word "indeterminateness" in regard to the size of the wage fund.

The doctrine Thornton had tried to controvert, though true, was not the whole truth. "He has shown," said Mill, "and has been the first to show, that there are cases which it does not reach."

### The crucial point

This brings us to the crucial point in the whole of Mill's argument.

> If it should turn out [he wrote] that the price of labour falls within one of the excepted cases—the case which the law of equality between demand and supply does not provide for, because several prices all agree in satisfying that law—we are able to see that the question between one of these prices and another will be determined by causes which operate strongly against the labourer, and in favour of the employer.

After discussing this possibility he remembered the "If" and wrote: "It will of course be said that these speculations are idle, for labour is not in that barely possible excepted case." That is just what would occur to one and what one would expect him to prove. But he made no attempt at a proof. Instead, he went off into a criticism of the wage-fund doctrine and, leaping over an immense logical gap, wrote:

> There is no law of nature making it inherently impossible for wages to rise to the point of absorbing not only the funds which he had intended to devote to carrying on his business, but the whole of what he allows for his private expenses, beyond the necessaries of life.

He obviously believed that in having shown that the conception of fixed limits to the wage fund was erroneous he had shown that a huge range of indeterminateness existed, the exact limits of which he defined more carefully later as

> the highest wages consistent with keeping up the capital of the country and increasing it *pari passu* with the increase of the people, and the lowest that will enable the labourers to keep up their numbers with an increase sufficient to provide labourers for the increase of employment.

This compares strangely with the moderation of his earlier generalization: "There is some amount of indeterminateness in its action, a certain limited amount of variation is possible within the bounds of the law." Thus, with no possible justification of any kind, with absolutely no logical foundation whatever, he declared that Thornton had shown that

> the doctrine hitherto taught by all or most economists (including himself) which denied it to be possible that trade unions can raise wages...is deprived of its scientific foundation and must be thrown aside.

## Diagrammatic treatment

There were similar ideas, as has been mentioned, in an essay by Fleeming Jenkin published before Thornton's book. After Mill's article had appeared and after a correspondence with Jevons, Jenkin developed his ideas in a further essay, and it is probable that, through its influence on Edgeworth (and Jevons), his work had more to do with the perpetuation of the idea of indeterminateness than Mill's.

Already, in 1868, Jenkin had expressed the equation of supply and demand algebraically, and in 1870 he introduced, independently of the then forgotten Cournot, and Dupuit, the device of supply and demand curves. It is not hard to imagine that such a writer should have profoundly interested the leading mathematical economist of the past generation. Edgeworth gave the two essays most enthusiastic praise, and as it was he who, more than any other thinker, elaborated the theory of indeterminateness, we can probably trace the cause to Jenkin.

He (Jenkin) illustrated by supply and demand curves Thornton's example of price in an auction, to which we have already referred, and showed that it really made the simple assumption that demand in the neighborhood of the market price was constant at all prices; that is, the demand curve became horizontal[11] near the market price and, owing to the supply curve also being level (one quantity offered singly and without reserve), the actual market price would be indeterminate. He described the diagram as representing "an unusual state of mind." This is putting it mildly indeed. It depends entirely upon the fortuitous coincidence of the horizontal section of an unusual and highly improbable curve with an absolutely rigid supply curve.

---

[11]He represented prices on the horizontal axis.

Had the supply been larger or smaller to any noticeable extent, even in this example, the price would have been theoretically determinate. Developing this idea and, it seems, getting further away from economic realities, he said:

> Where only a small number of transactions take place there can...be no theoretical market price; thus, with one buyer and seller of one thing, the demand and supply curves become two straight lines....If the supply line overlaps the demand line, the sale will take place, and not otherwise; but the price is indeterminate.[12]

### *Edgeworth developed the idea, but later on seems to have doubted its importance*

This was the idea that Edgeworth developed and the one that led him to make the remark already quoted, possibly inspired by the similar remark by Mill to the effect that the old belief that trade unions could not raise wages had to be given up. We cannot here discuss the detailed development of the idea in his hands. His chief contribution to the theory was to draw curves of indifference for two bargainers, thus representing graphically the area of indeterminateness. But he did not, any more than did Mill, show that there was any justification for considering the value of labor as specially influenced by this principle, or that it disclosed any increment of the total product of industry which could be diverted to those who provided labor.

We cannot be certain as to how far the Edgeworth of 1891 would have upheld the point of view expressed in 1881, for in a criticism of Marshall's "Note on Barter" (the "Note on Barter" appeared in the second edition of Marshall's *Principles*), he said, after an analysis of ideas of which he was the chief original propagator, that in comparison with other conditions of the labor market, they were "of little practical importance." In his own words:

> I do not, however, regard these nice points as more than *curiosa*, of little practical importance in comparison with the conditions of the labour market on which Marshall has dwelt.

He referred here to

---

[12]Fleeming Jenkin, *Collected Papers,* p. 85.

> the tendency of any accidental disadvantage under which the work-people may be suffering to become perpetuated through the lowering of their vitality and efficiency.[13]

This, however, is an entirely different point. Edgeworth had completely changed the basis of his defense of unionism. That same year, in his introductory lecture on political economy at Oxford, he said:

> As an instance in which eminent theorists may have omitted a relevant circumstance, may be taken the question whether it is possible for trade unionists, by standing out for a higher than the market rate of wages, to benefit themselves permanently without injuring other workmen. The negative answer which has sometimes been given omits the consideration that an increase of wages tends to increase efficiency...etc.

This deliberately avoids a reference to the affirmative answer which he had given ten years previously. In Sidgwick's *Principles,* Mr. L. L. Price's *Industrial Peace,* and Professor A. C. Pigou's *Principles and Methods of Industrial Peace,* the idea *seems* to have survived with more importance than Edgeworth would himself have attached to it.

### Mr. Flux has doubted its importance

We can detect in other economists who have dealt with the question the same doubt as to the importance of the idea. Mr. Flux, for example, discussing the alleged indeterminate increment, in 1900[14] wrote:

> Now, it can not be denied that this element is in existence in fact. The question rather is, whether it has sufficient generality, and whether the relative importance of the amounts involved is such as may entitle it to figure prominently in a discussion of the general problem of distribution.[15]

### Marshall's treatment

The later treatment of the idea by Marshall is very uncertain compared to his earlier treatment of it. He was possibly the

[13]Edgeworth, *Papers Relating to Political Economy,* vol. 2, p. 319.

[14]*Econ. Jour.,* 1900, p. 381.

[15]Compare Edgeworth's review of Davidson's "Bargain Theory of Wages" in the *Economic Journal,* 1899.

first to give an even superficially satisfactory explanation of why the value of labor should be considered as specially influenced by this principle. Basing his treatment on Edgeworth's conception, he illustrated it by considering the extremely artificial case of the barter, in isolation, of nuts and apples. In such an example he had no difficulty in showing "the uncertainty of the rate at which equilibrium is reached." It is what we should expect in a case of simple barter. But in the earlier editions of his *Principles* he said that this uncertainty

> does not depend on the fact that one commodity is being bartered for another instead of being sold for money. It results from our being obliged to regard the marginal utilities of both commodities as varying [third edition, p. 415].

It was *this* consideration that caused him to regard the price as likely to be indeterminate and arrived at *as* under barter, although in fact, not a subject of barter.

After his general treatment of the temporary equilibrium of demand and supply he remarked:

> We did not allow for any appreciable change in the marginal utility of money...[which is] justifiable with regard to most of the markets with which we are practically concerned.... The exceptions are rare and unimportant in markets for commodities; but in markets for labour they are frequent and important. When a workman is in fear of hunger, the marginal utility of money to him is very high; and if at starting he gets the worst of the bargaining and is employed at low wages, it remains low, and he may go on selling his labour at a low rate [third edition, pp. 411, 412].

This led him to his discussion of the barter of nuts and apples with a view to "throwing additional light" on the problem. In spite of the contention by Edgeworth that this treatment of "the specific peculiarities of the labour market...left little to be said freshly,"[16] we find Marshall's doubts expressed in subsequent changes of text. In a later edition he had substituted throughout for the workmen's "marginal utility of money," "his need of money (its marginal utility to him)" (seventh edition). This is a strange amendment, for whilst the word "need" is vague, "marginal utility" is definite. He probably felt that the phrase "*his* marginal utility" did not quite fit the case.

[16]*Econ. Jour.,* 1899, p. 231.

However, in a later edition he had relegated his "Note on Barter" to the appendix and omitted the phrase which claimed that it threw "additional light" on the labor market. (Compare p. 412, third edition, and p. 336, seventh edition). This also suggests a change of attitude. But his amendment to the "Note on Barter" was such as amounted to a tacit renunciation of the whole previous argument. Instead of contending that indeterminateness "does not depend on the fact that one commodity is being bartered for another instead of being sold for money," he seemed completely to reverse his previous contention, and said that it

> depends indirectly on the fact that one commodity is being bartered for another instead of being sold for money... the steadying influences which hold together a market in which values are set in money are absent [seventh edition, p. 793].[17]

All the amended argument of the later editions comes to is this: that where there is buying and selling through the agency of money there is more likely to be an effective market. Absence of money economy is one factor which may cause market forces to be ineffective.

### Under competition the marginal utilities of "income" or "money" are irrelevant

Having made the uncertainty of the equilibrium rates depend upon barter (and ultimately, though not *expressly* stated, upon the absence of an effective market), and peculiarities of labor in respect of the marginal utility of money become irrelevant. We get back to the position that Longfield discussed a century ago. An individual worker's need for income might be so great that he would be prepared to give 19/20ths of the results of his labor to the person who would lend him a spade rather than till the soil with his hands. But the market rate might be such that he might have to give only 1/5th. It is quite true that the poorer a workman is, the higher will be the marginal utility to him of further increments of income—that is, of those commodities in

---

[17]The word "indirectly" seems the wrong one. If he had said "generally" it would have been more true; for indeterminateness can exist where all transactions take place through the monetary mechanism.

general which satisfy his needs; but whilst it is clear that that will affect the intensity or amount of his efforts to get further income we have no reason at all to suppose that it will

(a) prevent in any way the formation of an effective market for his labor,

(b) cause an equilibrium in the market at a lower rate than would result from the same quantity of labor being offered by workers to whom the marginal utilities of income were lower.

### *Jevons's treatment in* The Theory of Political Economy

With Jevons the theory developed in a rather different way. Like Edgeworth he seems to have been influenced by Thornton and Jenkin. The latter had corresponded with him on the subject of the mathematical treatment of economics before publishing his second article, and it was partly in consequence of Jenkin's essays that Jevons decided to put his own *Theory of Political Economy* into print as early as 1871.

The idea emerged in his treatment of the theory of exchange. He put forward the proposition that

> the equation of exchange will fail to be possible when the commodity or useful article possessed on one or both sides is indivisible... [as, for instance, in the case of a house[18]] because we cannot contemplate the existence of an increment or decrement to an indivisible article[19].... The theory seems to give a very unsatisfactory answer, for the problem proves to be, within certain limits, indeterminate.

Such a bargain, he said, "must be settled upon other than strictly economic grounds." What *would* determine the result was "the comparative amount of knowledge of each other's *position* and *needs* (my italics) which each bargainer may possess." The only meaning I can suggest for this phrase is that the seller will endeavor to find out how the utility to be derived by the prospective buyer from the house compares with the utility he can derive by spending an equal amount in available

[18] The example of the sale of an estate was discussed in a not dissimilar manner in T. J. Dunning's *Trade Unions and Strikes,* 1859, p. 6.

[19] As a matter of fact, it is very easy to conceive of an increment to a house, as, indeed, of most other large properties.

alternative ways. What one is prepared to give for any commodity (or increment of a commodity) is a function of alternatives or alternative sources of supply. But Jevons was tacitly
assuming that there *were* no alternative sources of supply of
houses.

The case is similar to the theoretically isolated transaction
which we saw Longfield had dismissed as of no practical importance. It rests on three assumptions—largeness of unit,
uniqueness, and monopoly. The general unimportance of the
idea is further brought out in his elaboration of it. He held that
indeterminateness existed even when commodities were divisible, if their divisibility was not into infinitely small quantities.
As an illustration, he took bottles of ink. A fixed price (presumably competitive) of one shilling each was given, and the
indeterminateness thrown on to quantity—that is, the number
of bottles purchased at that price. Would the last and doubtful
one be purchased? Here, again, these hypothetical transactions
are isolated both in space and time. Putting aside the absence
of competing ink supplies, or supplies available in different-
sized units, when we take the factor of *time* into account, we
see that the size of the unit purchased at a particular transaction loses all its relevance and importance. We can only imagine the size of the bottles affecting the interval between pur-
chases—not the amount of ink consumed. This has an obvious
parallel, as we shall see, in the case of the supply of some kinds
of capital equipment.

*The danger of generalizing from isolated cases, and
ignoring the time factor in those cases*

Most of the erroneous deductions which have sprung out of
the indeterminateness conception appear to have arisen from
the expansion to a generalization of the results of a particular
isolated case. Mr. Flux, in reviewing Mr. J. A. Hobson's *Economics of Distribution,* based on ideas similar to those which I
have just discussed, remarked:

> That the gradations of any actual supply or demand schedule do
> not proceed by the infinitesimal changes assumed in the
> mathematical treatment of the problems of value may be
> granted. It need not follow that the gradations, though finite, are

of a magnitude requiring as much attention as demanded in the book under discussion.[20]

The important consideration, however, is not the size of units or gradations of supply and demand as affecting the size of transactions, but the influence of the time element, which causes the normal competitive economic forces to be effective.

### *Jevons's treatment in* The State in Relation to Labour

The treatment of bargains over large units was similar in Jevons's later work, *The State in Relation to Labour* (1882), but he substituted for comparative "knowledge of each other's position and needs" the "combat of desires and fears" of the parties, a combat which, he thought, was "only solved by the lapse of time which tries the patience of both parties." In view of the apparent similarity of this position to that which exists in the case of a strike it seems desirable to examine the idea.

In any *actual* case we should not find complete isolation, monopoly, and uniqueness; and the term "combat" is not quite satisfactory. Both parties may be extremely keen to secure the exchange of the property on good terms; and if the sum of money involved is a large one, afraid of misjudging the value of the investment or realization. The reason why the would-be *seller* waits is so that he may test the market. The possible purchasers at any one moment of an indivisible property of large value may be very small, but there are potential purchasers who will, in course of time, come into the market. The seller's judgment of the probable extent of potential demand will determine the price he will be prepared to accept. His inclination will most likely be to agree to a lower price in the present than he believes he will probably be offered in the future because, in so doing, he will discount both time and risk. The reason why the *buyer* waits is that he believes there *is* no other buyer who is likely, within a reasonable space of time, to offer the price he is prepared to pay; or that by waiting he can find an equally good alternative at that price. As both are keen to make a transaction both are aware of some loss to themselves in delay. They will sooner or later be in a position to

[20]*Econ. Jour.,* 1900, p. 381.

estimate whether their judgment was right or wrong and ultimately arrive at a price representing a rough coincidence of interest. Both parties may endeavor to "bluff"—that is, to create a false impression of the state of the market or their relationship to it—but the word "patience" explains nothing. If they had the means of forecasting the ultimate or long-run demand or supply, they would be relieved of the burden of waiting as a means of obtaining an indication of the position.

### *Jevons held that trade unions could not obtain general and permanent increases of wages*

Although obviously influenced by Thornton and Jenkin, Jevons did not indicate in his *Theory of Political Economy* that he thought the conception of indeterminateness was particularly applicable to the problem of labor's remuneration. That the idea may have been in his mind is suggested by the interpolation (almost as an afterthought) of the phrase: "It may be that indeterminate bargains of this kind" (e.g., over the sale of a house) "are best arranged by an arbitrator or third party"—an idea which is interesting in view of the later development of this idea by himself and others[21] in particular reference to labor.

It was only after the appearance of *Mathematical Psychics,* however, that Jevons ventured to follow Edgeworth in arguing that the existence of combinations in trade disputes usually reduces them to a single contract bargain of the same indeterminate kind. He made the application to labor in his *State in Relation to Labour,* a treatise which appeared in April 1882, a very short time after the publication of Edgeworth's book. The idea appears in the last chapter and seems rather in contradiction to the argument of the earlier chapters. There are, therefore, some grounds for a suspicion that it was hurriedly inserted. We certainly never get the impression from Jevons, as from Edgeworth, that the creation or magnifying of such indeterminateness by combinations was "favourable to the unionists," or that owing to the neglect by economists of like considerations "the untutored mind of the workman had gone

---

[21]Especially by Professor Pigou: "It is only because there is a margin of indeterminateness that the possibility and the need of [arbitration] exists" (*Principles and Methods of Industrial Peace,* p. 36).

more straight to the point than economic intelligence."[22] On the contrary, he had concluded

> that it is quite impossible for trades unions in general to effect any permanent increase in wages,[23] [and that there were] two possible modes of increasing earnings: the one being to increase products, so as to have more to sell, and the second to decrease products in order to sell them at a higher price.

Moreover, it followed "inevitably that if many or all people pursued the latter policy it would fail altogether."[24]

> Obviously...,[he said] the rate of wages which workmen can demand will depend upon the relation of supply to demand of such particular kind of labour.[25]

*Jevons rejected the supply and demand theory of wages and brought in "indeterminateness"*

The remarkable thing is that the whole of the point of view here expressed, in fact, the complete argument of his chapter 4, is, in chapter 7 on "Arbitration and Conciliation," casually superseded in a couple of pages (pp. 153–55) as being mere abstraction, an analysis of what would have been the case if things had been different from what, in reality, they were.

> The existence, however, of combinations in the labour market [he wrote] alters the nature of the bargains altogether. The laws of supply and demand do not apply to such a case. In all bargains about a single object there may arise, as I have explained in my *Theory of Political Economy,* a deadlock.

What he failed to show was that such examples could be linked in any useful way to the problem of bargains between combinations of capital and labor. Even if we could accept his assumption that they might be validly regarded as bargaining about a single object, there would still exist this radical difference, that whereas a contract over the sale of a house or an estate is a contract presumably for perpetuity, agreements between capital and labor are capable of being subjected to constant recontract.

---

[22]*Mathematical Psychics.*
[23]Jevons, *The State in Relation to Labour,* 1882, p. 106.
[24]Ibid., p. 94.
[25]Ibid., p. 93.

But *can* bargains between combinations of capital and labor be legitimately regarded as concerned with anything resembling "a single object" or, as he had expressed it in his earlier book, "an indivisible object"? Surely, it is almost impossible to imagine anything more easily divisible than labor supplied. The two sides may haggle about the price per unit of labor but not about the amount of available labor that will be taken on at any given price. The price of labor will very rarely be immaterial to capitalists (even as perfect monopolists) in determining how much labor they can profitably employ, for instance. Each party may rely, however, on some immobility, temporary or permanent, of the factor of production owned by the other, causing a certain rigidity in the response of quantity to price; and Jevons might have extended his argument to cover this class of case. Instead, he introduced what seems at first a new consideration to explain indeterminateness—that is, the disutility of strikes and lockouts to the parties.

### *Political economy is not "silenced" under bilateral monopoly*

> The men, for instance, [he wrote] ask for fifteen per cent advance of wages all round. Rather than have a strike, it might be for the interest of employers to give the advance or for the men to withdraw their demand; *a fortiori* any intermediate arrangement would still more meet their views.

As in the case of the house transaction in his *Theory of Political Economy,* he argued that there may be "absolutely no economic principle on which to decide the question." The disutilities of strikes and lockouts can, of course, be paralleled with the loss from delay in that illustration, but a comparison is misleading. In the case of labor there is no inability to test the market through the absence of small increments; and the continuous refusal to contract in this case seems to be a delay with an entirely different motive. Even if we neglect "motives," we still cannot make a parallel, for in the former case the passage of time reveals the market or alternatives, whereas in the latter the very factors which normally reveal the market are suppressed.

The object of the strike or lockout when initiatory seems to be to obtain a price higher or lower than available alternatives to both parties would determine, and the power to do so ultimately rests upon control of alternatives—that is, upon the power to exploit monopoly. There are many elements of uncertainty in the determination of price in such circumstances. Apart from those which we have already noticed, the factors determining the extent of control or limitation in any case may be complex and uncertain, and hence the result unpredictable from this cause. The prices resulting may favor one party or the other, but there is no reason why we should say that economic principle fails to work; or as economists so careful as Sidgwick and, following him, Mr. L. L. Price, have held, that "where two combinations meet one another, political economy is perforce silenced."[26] Professor Macgregor has pointed out in his *Industrial Combinations* that

> relative fewness tends to introduce elements which are more psychological than economic, though they can scarcely be called accidental to an economic analysis.[27]

Judgment, of course, is less certain when transactions are few and potential demand and supply have to be estimated; and "bluff" may admittedly come in. These elements, it seems, are the only psychological ones which *mere fewness* necessarily brings in. Moreover, economic principle applies with equal relevance to conditions of relative monopoly as to conditions of relative competition. Not only is there no clear line of division between the two, but, to use Professor Davenport's words,

> It may indeed by said that in the main competitive and monopoly theory do not diverge, that the supply and demand analysis applies without change to monopoly and that monopoly differs from competition only in the fact that in monopoly the volume of supply is under centralised control, while in competition the limit of supply is found in marginal cost of production.[28]

## Monopolist control of supply may be direct or through price control

Monopoly power rests ultimately upon the ability to limit or control supply. Such limitation or control may be direct—that

[26]L. L. Price, *Economic Science and Practice,* p. 192. (Also in his *Industrial Peace.*)

[27]*Industrial Combinations,* pp. 69-70.

[28]*Economics of Enterprise,* p. 482.

is, scarcities may be created to suit the interests of particular groups by direct restriction or exclusion (and much trade-union action is of this nature); or such limitation may be in- direct—that is, monopolists may proceed by enforcing certain prices which suit them. It is combined resistance to attempts of the latter kind to enforce adverse prices that usually causes strikes or lockouts to continue for more than one moment of time.

### Strikes and lockouts best regarded as "coercive devices"

The problems we have just been considering are perhaps made clearer if we regard strikes and lockouts (whether ag- gressive or defensive is immaterial) as *coercive devices*. Like a similar coercive weapon, "the boycott," they may be employed for a variety of motives and for the attainment of many dif- ferent ends. They are a deliberate interference with the free and continuous flow of the services of the workers, capital equip- ment, or other factor of production in response to a given economic condition, competitive or monopolistic. Their object is generally either to force another party to acquiesce in a price other than the competitive or to resist such a price which another party seeks to impose.

As we have already seen, the mere grouping in combinations of the owners of cooperant resources such as "property" and "labor" would not necessarily cause indeterminateness, pro- vided transactions were made in small units. It is the joint determination by one group not to let another make contracts with individuals among them, which, judged by their available alternatives, would be most favorable to them, that creates the range of indeterminateness and the conditions in which a strike is possible; the determination that *all* transactions shall be made at a certain price (or more favorable ones) or there will be no transactions at all. For this reason we have additional grounds for saying that there is definitely a *"coercive"* element in such actions.

The institution of property gives all monopolists the power to prevent access by other factors of production to the resources that they control. By that means the formation of a true socially determined price is prevented and a private coercion is substituted for a social coercion. (The meaning of "social coercion" is given below.) In the *absence* of monopoly, the institution of property may be held to be the very institution which causes the various factors of production to move to the most profitable channels as determined by society. In its *presence,* that view cannot be held.[29]

### *Successful strikes and lockouts establish a private coercion in place of a social coercion*

Where there is a complete absence of monopoly all individuals dealing in small increments are powerless in regard to price. They may give goods away, but we cannot call such happenings "transactions." Except in ignorance, or as a gift, or as a method of aggession to secure concessions, selling below or buying above the market price is inconceivable under perfect competition. Hence, when the market is the ruling force, we have what might be called "a social coercion," the impartial and impersonal ruling of society itself expressed in the resultant of those forces which make up the market. (The term "coercion" may seem the wrong word, for in this case it is definitely a product of the utmost freedom and mobility.) The monopolist aims at substituting for this socially determined price one that is believed to favor a particular group; and the power to do so is definitely obtained from a coercive power over individual cooperating units, preventing them from exercising that freedom which, under competition, results in the controlling power of market price.

### *This explains the "range of indeterminateness"*

We can now come back to the idea of the range of indeterminateness. Is not the best explanation of it to be found in the

[29]This must not, of course, be taken as implying a condemnation of "large" properties. In the community of the world a very large property indeed may, through direct competition and that of substitutes and alternatives, be quite unable to exploit any monopoly power at all. But the usual defense of private property on economic grounds does not necessarily hold in such cases. That defense presupposes the most complete mobility and responsiveness of every unit of resources. It is only when this mobility and responsiveness exists that there can be any *certain* validity in what is thought to be a common assumption of economists that the price determined under private enterprise is the one which best serves the common good.

fact that under bilateral monopoly you have two groups with coercive power of this kind, each attempting in the case of a strike to enforce a price against the interest of the other? The result may not be predictable, nor may the forces determining the ultimate price be expressible in schedules, but political economy is not "silenced." Quite apart from the economic nature of the coercive power, both parties will adjust their supply or demand according to the ruling price exactly as they would if the price had been fixed by the free market or legal enactment; and this remains the case, as we shall see, *although the actual division of the spoils of monopoly obtained at the expense of the consumer is largely an arbitrary affair;* and the limits to which either party will go will be influenced by the possibility of revision of the terms and other expected long-run reactions of their policy.

### Can monopoly gains be made at the expense of the owners of other factors of production?

Having considered the nature of the strike and monopoly coercion, we can now tackle the question of whether, by the exploitation of monopoly, the owners of one factor of production as a whole may gain at the expense of another—labor at the expense of the owners of property, for instance, or vice versa. (These groups are, of course, not naturally exclusive. Most property owners receive incomes from work and most "workers" own *some* property.)

### Particular groups may gain by excluding other factors when they are competitive

Any *group* of persons together owning some portion of the factors of production may gain by keeping out of supply (or operation) certain factors of production owned by others; that is, they may gain as producers and sellers of certain commodities by preventing increments of factors owned by others, which might add to the supply of those commodities, from coming in to cooperate in the task of production. In so far as they can thus exclude, the total product (not necessarily its aggregate value) will be smaller. Thus their gain will be accompanied partly by loss to those excluded from cooperating in the task, and partly by loss to those who buy the commodity, who will have to pay a higher price per unit for the smaller quantity.

What factors it will pay any particular group to exclude will depend upon several considerations. Other things being equal, it will certainly pay the workers in any particular case to exclude such factors as capital equipment or new methods of organization when they are "labor-saving," i.e., when their exclusion will mean that more workers can be employed at the same rate of wages or the same number at a higher rate of wages. In other cases, the exclusion of capital equipment, improved organization or other factor will result in a fall in demand for the workers themselves (although they might not realize this), and a gain to them is *not* certain. In regard to other supplies of like factors, however (workers of the same type, for example), exclusion will nearly always benefit the *particular group* practicing it: and the gain will have been at the expense of the owners of the units excluded, and accompanied by loss to the consumer and probably to other factors of production.

### "At the expense of"

Before going further we need to devote some attention to the phrase "at the expense of." Any monopolist-gain by a single monopolist among cooperant producing groups is necessarily accompanied by loss to certain of the other groups, for one reason because at the higher price asked by the monopoly factor there is, even in the absence of direct exclusion, some fall in the number of units of it demanded, and a consequent fall in the number of units of work or service demanded from the factors of production which cooperate with it. Thus, a trade union exclusion of competing workmen from a particular job tends to make both the capitalist and the consumer worse off. We might therefore say that the trade union gains at the expense of excluded workers, capital, and the consumer.

Yet, in a discussion such as this, mainly concerned with the possibility of redistribution, it might be convenient to distinguish broadly between
  (1) the source of those gains to one party which are possible
      because of the nature or condition of a factor of produc-

tion owned by some other party, that is, when it is "exploitable" or "excludable," and

(2) those losses to owners of other factors which are incidental rather than direct, although not necessarily unimportant.

For instance, there is usually no point in a labor monopoly excluding directly a body of noncompeting but cooperant workers (i.e., those engaged on an entirely different, complementary process), for they will be worse off by so doing. But *any* exclusion which pays them may, incidentally, exclude *some* noncompeting workers. We can distinguish here between the loss to those whom *it has paid* to exclude and the loss to those who also happen to be kept out by that policy. The gain may be said to be obtained by the exclusion of the former (although also accompanied by loss to the latter, but not by their exploitation, for it would be impossible to gain at their expense alone). And, again, monopoly profits which are obtainable by any factor solely because of inelasticity of demand for the commodity by the consumer, may be said to exploit him, although the other factors of production as a whole *may* be worse off as a result of the exploitation of that monopoly. Monopoly profits to a factor which are possible solely owing to immobility of other factors may be said to be obtained by exploiting them, although as a result of their exploitation the consumer is worse off. This use of the term "exploit" is purely for convenience; it makes no clear logical distinction,[30] and it is not implied that these "incidental losses," as we have called them, are not highly important. Almost invariably monopoly gains, no matter to what factor, are accompanied by loss to the consumer.

*A group of workers may gain without exclusion against an inelastic demand*

For the next stage of our argument it will be most useful to take first a particular case and ask: Is it possible for a group of workers to gain without exclusion of other workers? If so, by whose exploitation may we say they have gained?

---

[30]The elasticity of supply of any "nonexploitable" cooperant factor in this sense will influence the degree to which it is desirable to exploit any other cooperant factor or the consumer.

Let us assume first that all other factors are in competition among themselves. When the relationship of the workers to other factors of production and the demand for the commodity is such that the number of units of their labor demanded is inelastic to rises in their remuneration per unit (from whatever cause), the restriction of the amount offered by them at a price may mean a larger aggregate return to them. In other words, by forcing a price higher than the competitive, and practicing work-sharing or a restriction of output, every worker in the group may be better off than under competition, although no workers whom competitive remuneration would have attracted have been excluded. This appears to be what the Webbs mean when (in dealing with Edgeworth's contention on this point that combined parties tend to gain at the expense of uncombined parties with whom they are dealing) they say: "Nor need the combination amount in any sense to a monopoly." (*Industrial Democracy*, p. 653.) The action is, of course, essentially monopolistic, although not necessarily to be condemned on that account if it does result in a redistribution of the product of industry in favor of the relatively poor.

> Because the total produce is diminished, it does not follow that the labourer's share is diminished (the loss may fall on the capitalist and entrepreneur whose compressibility has been well shown by Mr Sidgwick). [Edgeworth, *Mathematical Psychics.*]

### Is restriction of output to the interests of the workers?

But does an examination of this hypothetical possibility enable us to say, as Edgeworth said in regard to the alleged disbelief of trade unionists in the wage fund, that in the matter of the *work fund*

> the untutored mind of the workman had gone more straight to the point than economic intelligence misled by a bad method, reasoning without mathematics upon mathematical subjects?

Does the road to plenty for the workers lie in restriction, worksharing, and "short time"?[31]

---

[31] When a fund such as "unemployment donation" (provided by state or charity) exists to remunerate workers excluded, the whole body of workers may *conceivably* gain as a whole. But this represents a direct transference of society's income which *could* have been effected equally well without trade union action, the resulting unemployment and its incidental loss.

*Gains of this kind rare in practice*

Attempts to obtain pure gains of this nature seem to be very rare in practice. We find few cases of conscious and rational worksharing. Trade-union officials think in terms of rates per head—not aggregates. There may, nevertheless, be some increment of this sort of gain combined with the gain from direct exclusion when unions are faced with an inelastic demand. If we allow for conditions which cause a certain inertia in the movement of economic factors, the conclusion suggests itself that inelastic demand for labor is ultimately very rare.

The question of the demand for labor in general raises big difficulties which cannot be dealt with here. But from broad considerations of this kind we might, whilst frankly admitting the possibility of large gains to particular groups, deny the likelihood of any general improved redistribution between different factors of production or income classes. This would not satisfy the skeptic, however, and accordingly the following analysis is desirable.

*We cannot assume elasticity of demand for labor where other factors are cooperant and not competitive*

To the extent to which a considerable part of the other factors (e.g., capital equipment) can be "labor saving," the condition of inelasticity is unlikely to exist even in the short run, because of the possibility of substitution. When, on the other hand, the marginal increments of other factors are cooperant rather than competing in their relation to labor, we cannot *assume* probable elasticity of demand.

*The possibility of ultimate gain by artificial wage rates depends upon the elasticity of demand for the product*

When a group of workers raises the price per unit of its work and adopts the device of work sharing, the effect is that in supplying less units for the process of production they have allowed less units of the other factors to cooperate; that is, they have excluded or caused to remain idle that portion of those factors which no longer finds its most profitable use in that field. They must be able either to prevent such excluded units of other factors from cooperating with other supplies of workers whom earnings above the competitive level in the particular trade would tend to attract, or to rely upon such cooperation being, for other reasons, impossible. As we have assumed that other factors are in competition the *ultimate* effect will be that increased costs will cause a diversion of the resources comprising those factors until the return to the marginal increment of each category thereof has fallen to normal. *When this has resulted,* it seems extremely improbable that the workers will have gained unless the demand for the commodity is inelastic. The elasticity of demand for the commodity will determine the price obtained by the competitive sellers for the smaller product, and hence the extent to which other resources will be driven away by the increased costs.

A gain resulting from *this* circumstance, therefore, cannot be said to be obtained by exploiting property or any other factor, for only the nature of the demand for the product enables it to be realized. It is obtained by exploiting the consumer.

### Until cooperant factors can move they may be exploited

Any monopoly increment accruing to the workers' group which does *not* result from this circumstance must arise from the fact that the diversion of other factors of production referred to above may be slow. Some resources we can conceive of as being transferred immediately there is any increase of costs, but there might be a long lag with others for which there are no sufficiently profitable alternative uses. The whole question turns principally on the elasticity of supply of other factors, which it is now convenient in view of current terminology to lump together under one heading as "capital." The supply of capital we must regard as being, *in the long run,* highly elastic. In respect of some forms of it, particularly new capital coming forward, it is obviously so; but in some other concerns, particularly those with large fixed plants, it seems at first sight to be the very reverse.

### Factors making for short-run immobility of "capital"

In the short run, the elasticity of demand for labor of a particular concern is almost always inelastic. It may have, for instance, a contract to fulfill and be under a penalty for failure. In such circumstances a labor combination might demand and obtain a rise of 50 percent in wages, and yet the numbers employed, even if the job had to be carried on at a loss, hardly fall off at all. It is perhaps in part owing to the ease with which gains may be made in this way at the expense of the entrepreneur that the terms of contracts often have a clause inserted to the effect that in the case of any changes in the remuneration of labor an adjusting modification of the price payable shall be made.

There are many other kinds of short-run commitments the existence of which may make for temporary inelasticity of demand. Probably the most important of all is the necessity to pay interest on capital or on borrowed money where there are heavy overhead costs. Undertakings such as railways or other public works, in which capital consists largely in valuable plant and equipment that cannot be turned to other uses, are the outstanding example of this. At first, it seems that we have here a case in which labor can exploit capital, if not permanently, at least over a long period; and where demand is not expanding, capital *does* appear to be definitely exploitable. Yet, even in the extreme case of absolute immobility of capital, we can conceive of factors likely to cause some degree of elasticity. Quite apart from the possible substitution of labor-saving equipment, new means of economizing labor are almost certain to become profitable when it is more expensive.

*Apparent exploitability of immobile factors may prove illusory*

In practice, for many reasons, when considerable rises in general costs cannot be passed on to the consumer, *some* part of the total capital equipment will be closed down. There will most likely be a hard struggle before such action is considered, but as soon as it becomes clear that absolute loss cannot be avoided on the operation of a particular section of plant, then it will be laid idle. In such a case a new equilibrium will be *suddenly* realized after a time, and at a single moment a large number of workers may be at once dismissed. How soon such a result will follow any increase of costs will depend upon how near the unprofitable point the unit of plant involved happens to be before that increase. This suggests that in practice such elasticity of demand for labor as there is, is effective, so to speak, "in jerks." Increased wages which occasion little reduction in numbers employed might, if raised a little further, result in a considerable reduction. Hence, whereas it is theoretically possible, from the factors we have so far considered that, in particular cases, labor stands to gain, it must be remembered that whether the necessary theoretical conditions will be present or not in any case will be in some degree a matter of chance. Unless the true position is realized adequately in each case a rise in wages may often result in a large drop in numbers employed.

### When such policies become normal, no cooperant factor is exploitable

But however strong the probability that capital will be exploitable in such circumstances, we cannot validly generalize from the particular. If it were really normal for labor to exploit capital invested in this class of undertaking, the result would be that less would be invested in this class. Owing to the risk of such exploitation, capital would be diverted to channels which, through that risk, would become relatively profitable. New capital is absolutely mobile. Or, to put the matter in more general terms, resources are attracted to particular productive channels in the light of the claims on the value of the product made by cooperant factors. Where competition exists there is no expectation that the size of other claims will be permanent except for the contract period; but resources will only be directed into channels in which they must become immobile in the light of the probable future variation through competition of the terms demanded by the others. Where artificial interferences through monopoly or state regulations are general it is in the light of the expected course of *their* results that resources will be attracted. Thus, once collective bargaining or legal enactment becomes the normal policy, no cooperant factor of production is in itself exploitable.

### The size of the unit of supply is irrelevant

The size of the technical unit of supply makes no difference to this principle at all. The supply of plant that is only possible in large units reacts to intensification of demand in exactly the same way as does plant for industries of different form, except that it does so "in jerks." Thus, although a particular increase in wages costs may not result in a large falling off in numbers employed it may have prevented a large increase which was imminent. In practice, these considerations are somewhat masked by the fact that such concerns are themselves in some degree monopolistic and can withstand increased costs up to a point by placing a further burden on the consumer.

### Exploitation of "capital" a breach of faith with investors in immobile resources

The exploitation of capital by particular groups of workers is, thus, impossible except during the first transition from competition to monopoly or regulation; and such exploitation might be regarded as a breach of faith on the part of society with those who have chosen to invest in relatively immobile resources. We must, however, bear in mind that the probability of aggregate gain is, even in this class of case, not high (as we have seen above).

### "Labor" no more exploitable through immobility than "capital"

In the same way, the general exploitation of "labor" by "capital" through its immobility can be shown to be equally impossible. Once again, the question can be approached by considering elasticity of supply, which is probably greatest among laborers, the completely unspecialized class. Workers of this kind, although their territorial mobility may be small (in so far as they correspond to the most poorly paid class), have yet a wide range of alternative occupations. The chief restrictions on their mobility are those which have been created by labor organizations themselves and are clearly against the advantage of owners of capital generally. Here also, as with the supply of capital, in the very short run the supply of labor is inelastic and capable, in particular cases and during the first transition from competition to monopoly among capitalists, of temporary exploitation. But with the progress of modern industrial organization and technique and the growing tendency for labor to lose its specialization, as skill is thrown more and more on to the machine, the power even in these circumstances to obtain short-run gains through immobility becomes less and less possible.

In practice, for many reasons, reductions of wages sought for by capitalists involve relatively small percentages except in times of monetary disturbance when prices generally are fluctuating rapidly. Undue lowering of wages can be met by a gradual migration of the more efficient workers to the considerable disadvantage of the injudicious firm. There is no parallel in labor to the immobility of huge capital units.

*Deliberately imposed restrictions on mobility of labor*
*not advantageous to capital in general*

The principle remains the same even if, for the sake of argument, we suppose it to be possible for the capitalist to impose deliberate restrictions on the mobility of labor. In so far as a capitalist can, by any device, prevent his workers from moving to take advantage of the labor market elsewhere he can, it seems, obviously gain at their expense. The more effective his power, it appears, the greater will be his gain. Surely, it will be said, laws or institutions designed to keep agricultural workers on the land, for instance, will benefit the farming community in so far as they succeed. The answer is that more of the other resources of the country will remain in or flow into that form of enterprise. In cases where such restrictions have been imposed under changing conditions, and until a new equilibrium has been reached, and so long as competition from existing or potential farmers can be prevented, the profitableness of farming will be above the normal. But it hardly seems likely that suppression of competition would be possible in the case of so large a group, even for a short time. In any case it does not follow from this that labor in general will lose relatively to capital in general, even in the short run (including all other factors of production under the heading "capital"). For labor elsewhere will probably benefit through the relative scarcity of labor, and capitalists elsewhere lose through the same scarcity. Further analysis of this *unimportant* point would have to consider the effect of relative elasticities of demand for the different factors in competitive and noncompetitive channels. But this is a question on which we can formulate so few valid generalizations that it seems desirable to regard it as a chance consideration affecting the result.

### New labor coming forward is unexploitable even in the short run

The same reasoning applies in regard to incidental immobility, i.e., that which is not the result of deliberate contrivance. Where there has been temporary exploitation of an immobile labor group, workers in other groups will tend to lose, not to gain, as it is overcome; and capitalists elsewhere will tend to gain as labor becomes more plentiful to them. Trade-union demarcations and artificial restriction on entrance to different occupations, state regulation of wages, and generally policies which hinder labor transference—all tend to create the conditions in which exploitation of the kind we are considering may appear to be possible in particular cases. It seems that if a large number of occupations have their entrance restricted, openings for adequate alternative employment for those workers who feel themselves to be unfairly treated will be so limited that they will have to lower their supply price considerably in order to get absorbed. Such short-run monopoly gains *as* are possible to capitalists through the existence of such conditions must, of course, be offset by the monopoly gains of those groups of workers whose protective system alone enables the capitalist to exploit. But in regard to the constant flow of new labor coming forward, however irrational we may believe the choice of trades to be, we may yet presume that trades whose workers are being "exploited" by employers owing to their acquired or incidental immobility will be avoided.

### The consumer alone is ultimately exploitable by collective action

To sum up our main conclusions so far: we have seen that combined labor cannot be said to exploit the cooperant factors of production possessed by the capitalist, and that labor combinations do not enable workers in general to exploit capital in general. The ultimate gains of workers by combinations when not at the expense of excluded competitors are obtained by exploiting the consumer; for the extent to which capital will be excluded by decreased supply of labor at a higher cost per unit will depend upon elasticity of demand for the *commodity,* which will determine the margin which gives the normal rate of return. We have also seen that combined capital not practicing exclusion of those whom *competitive* profits would attract cannot be said to gain by exploiting the worker but by exploiting the consumer.

Briefly, the import of these conclusions may be summarized as follows:

No factor of production can maintain the cooperation of another factor by offering it or leaving it an amount of the product less than the value of its net product elsewhere. The extent to which demand for the product falls off as its price is raised determines the quantity of one factor that will be driven away by another factor getting a larger share. Hence, we can say that monopoly gains by any factor are ultimately obtained by exploiting the consumer, although incidental losses are usually thrown upon other cooperant factors.

### Why the erroneous belief has arisen

The widespread belief that monopoly gains (or gains by wage regulation) are obtainable by labor and capital at one another's expense seems to have arisen (1) from the belief that if any or all wage rates are raised artificially, workers as a whole will get more; and (2) from the habit of regarding "labor" and "capital" as in opposition rather than as cooperators in production.[32]

### Lower wage rates may mean higher aggregate earnings

The popular view ignores completely the possibility that the aggregate amount paid in wages might be increased by a shifting (directly or through recruitment) of workers from lower-paid to higher-paid jobs, even if there were many substantial

[32]In so far as they are *competitors* they may gain at one another's expense by excluding units of competing resources, e.g., successful labor opposition to labor-saving machinery, etc. It is not suggested that such a policy can be to the *general* advantage of either party. The reverse can be shown.

reductions in wage *rates* and (what would be unlikely to happen in practice) there was no corresponding rise in the less well paid jobs. Still less does the popular view take account of the increase in the aggregate welfare of the workers which would result from greater equality caused by such a redistribution.

### As the consumer is alone exploitable we expect to find and do find "joint monopolies"

The habit of regarding labor and capital as in opposition has been encouraged by economic textbooks. It may be convenient for some purposes to represent their relations to one another by supply and demand schedules, so long as it is not forgotten that the ultimate demand for both of them is the demand for their jointly produced product. As monopoly gains, both to workers' and to capitalists' combinations, are ultimately obtained solely by limiting the supply of the commodities, it is not surprising that we find joint monopolies, that is, different cooperant factors of production consciously or tacitly practicing monopoly together and dividing the spoils. A joint monopoly is a greatly strengthened one, and represents a concentration of interests against those excluded. It is a particular case of vertical combination (generally tacit).

Often, it will definitely pay an employers' monopoly that its employees shall combine. If there is any body of workers free to cooperate with a rival manufacturer whom monopoly prices would bring into the field the capitalist's monopoly is threatened; and this accounts for the frequent agreement between an employers' combination and a trade union for the payment of a high wage provided that the union will see that no workers at all in that occupation shall be employed at less. In modern times the state has intervened to strengthen such joint monopolies, either by making agreements arrived at by industrial councils binding on the trade or by direct legal enactment.

Combined workers themselves have nearly always encouraged their employers to combine also. They have been strong advocates of price agreements, have roundly condemned "cutthroat" competition, and have asked for state help to protect "the good employer." In joint monopoly is to be found the explanation of most trade-union action in these times, and of much capital combination at all times.

### The indeterminateness of "the quota"

There is always an arbitrary element in the division of monopoly spoils. In the case of the quota system with a capital monopoly, or a system of work sharing by a trade union, the problem is always there of deciding how many shall be allowed to participate at all. In the case of a trade union it will probably be the normal number employed before the exercise or further exercise of monopoly power. And then we get the problem of how *different kinds* of participants shall share in the proceeds. In the case of a group of workers engaged on the same process "the standard rate" usually settles the matter, although there may still be some grading according to ability. When we get two groups of workers sharing the monopoly but engaged on noncompeting or complementary (cooperant) processes, some formula roughly based on "justice" may be applied; for example, we may get the proceeds divided more or less in proportion to former competitive earnings, or supposed difficulty of the task or technical status, etc. There is, however, no certain exterior principle such as the market to refer to in this division: from some points of view it is a purely arbitrary affair. In regard to considerations which can be usefully expressed or represented in schedules or curves, the division among them is "indeterminate." As a rule, equal division per head of workers seems to be sufficiently just: they are seldom conscious of any serious divergence of interest between different groups. Yet, in essence, the problem of the division between workers of the monopoly increment is the same as in the case of joint monopoly between capital and labor.

### The advantage in collusion

Now joint monopolists may either act independently, or in collusion (deliberate or tacit). If they act independently and seek to maximize their own share of the monopoly gain, the aggregate gain will be, other things being equal, smaller than if they act in collusion. For in acting independently they will each restrict their contribution in response to the terms on which they can get the other factors to cooperate. If any one factor only is a monopolist, it will presumably so limit its contribution as to maximize the return to it, given what competition commands shall be paid to the other factors. Any increase in costs to that monopolized factor (whether due to monopoly of another factor or not is immaterial) will presumably cause it to reduce its contribution still further in order to maximize, not the aggregate received for the commodity, but its share of the total. As it is to the obvious advantage of all factors considered together that the greatest aggregate shall be obtained, we can say that each monopolist factor seeking its own end does not serve their general good. No matter what division of the proceeds finally results (within the range of indeterminateness), collusion in regard to output will benefit all factors, for no factor need get less and all may get more than under independent action. Hence, we may expect to find, and in practice we do find, some measure of tacit collusion, or forbearance and "reasonableness" among cooperant monopolistic groups.

### Joint monopoly in the early nineteenth century

It is impossible in this essay adequately to indicate the significance in economic history of joint monopoly of this kind. All that can be done is to suggest grounds for the belief that its importance has been greatly underestimated. It has already been pointed out that practically all the combinations among employers that were revealed by the inquiries in England in 1824 and 1825 were either retaliatory against unions exploiting "the strike in detail" or else the employers' side of joint monopolies operating with the encouragement and connivance of the workers. Francis Place merely wanted the Combination Laws repealed, and had no interest in bringing out the true significance of the evidence which was brought forward. His comment on an obvious case of joint monopoly was:

> Employers advised the men to combine. Thus it appears the law is so iniquitous that those in whose favour it was made encourage the men to break it.[33]

Even in the days when combinations were illegal there is much evidence of employers encouraging their men to combine. There seems to have been a good deal of it among the

---

[33]Note written on his copy of the *Report of the Select Committee on Artisans and Machinery,* 1824, p. 279.

Framework Knitters, directly fostered by the masters.[34] And we find just as frequently cases of organized workmen petitioning their employers and urging them to combine: the Journeymen Coach-Makers were trying during 1816 and 1817 to get their masters to organize.[35] The rules of the Journeymen Paper-Makers of 1823 included a doggerel verse beginning with the ominous words: "May masters with their men unite."[36] Other cases of joint monopoly (or attempts to protect the "honorable masters," as they were called) before 1824 were found among the Rochdale weavers,[37] the Stockport Cotton Spinners, the Dublin Saddlers, the Hosiers, the Shipwrights, the Calico Printers, and many other established trades of that day.[38] It was always the "honorable employers" whom they sought to protect; and the same phraseology remains today. In those early times they had even conceived of the utility of the device known today as "extension of agreements" which is found in conjunction with legislation concerning industrial councils and arbitration courts in so many parts of the world. In 1824 the Lace-Makers petitioned Sir J. Hobhouse to introduce a bill

> for regulating wages by the decisions of a board composed of selected masters and men, and making the scale thus agreed upon binding on the trade....[39]

He refused.

## Inadequate recognition of the significance of "joint monopoly"

The nineteenth century is full of further examples of joint monopoly. Yet, as already pointed out, it has received singularly little recognition except by casual comment of unimportant

---

[34]E.g., Evidence of Thorpe and Ben Taylor, *Report of Select Committee on Artisans and Machinery,* 1824, pp. 274, 281.

[35]Place Add. MSS. 27799: 147–48.

[36]*Report of Select Committee on Combination Laws,* 1825, p. 59.

[37]Ibid., p. 154.

[38]The Reports of the Committees of 1824 and 1825 already referred to are full of evidence, direct and indirect, on this point, as are also the Place MSS. and cuttings. We find the same phenomenon during the seventeenth and eighteenth centuries.

[39]Felkin, *History of the Machine Wrought Hosiery,* p. 344.

writers. A pamphlet in 1867 recognized that "the means which secure the workmen the monopoly of labour, secure the masters also from any heavy pressure of competition."[40] In 1905, a writer on *Employers' Associations* recognized that they were "but a logical step in, and the natural complement of, the trade-union movement," and that they were "an essential feature [of it] without which it would be impossible for it to accomplish the purposes for which it exists."[41]

But we seldom find so certain an understanding of this relation between employers' and workers' combinations. This is perhaps because *formal* combinations between capital and labor have been rare. In the late 1890s a number of open alliances of this kind were flourishing in England in certain hardware, furniture, and china trades. The leading advocate of this form of organization was one E. J. Smith, who had no very clear idea of the economic implications of the developments he advised. His schemes received the cordial approval of the *Economic Review* and were by no means regarded as against the general interest by the *Economic Journal*.[42] The injurious and monopolistic nature of such organizations was, however, pointed out by Professor Cannon[43] and by Professor Pigou.[44] About the same time similar organizations had grown up on the Continent—"Les Syndicats Mixtes" of France. None of these alliances resulted in very close bodies and they do not appear to have survived for long.

### Importance of joint monopoly in modern society

If open and deliberate alliances like these have been rare, cases of tacit mutual support of each other by capitalist and labor groups have been widespread, and are typical of modern economic society. They have been encouraged and developed by tariff and industrial legislation—especially by arbitration, conciliation, and wage regulation acts. In joint monopoly, the

---

[40]H. M. White, *The Principles of Trade Unionism*, 1867, p. 17.

[41]*Quarterly Journal of Economics*, 1905, p. 110.

[42]See paragraph, obviously written by Edgeworth, in *Econ. Jour.*, 1898, p. 227.

[43]*Econ. Jour.*, 1900, p. 63.

[44]*Principles and Methods of Industrial Peace.*

writer believes, we have the real clue to the understanding of "antisweating" movements, which have not yet, in his opinion, received adequate impartial study. In the present stage of development, when the size of the monopoly unit is tending to become larger, and when capitalist monopoly tendencies are made respectable by the adoption of the propagandist euphemism "rationalization,"[45] the same relationship is there on a larger scale. Dr. Robert Liefmann's proposal that trade-union representatives should be admitted to cartel directorates and that employers should have permanent representatives on trade-union executives is a good manifestation of it.

### The assumption of rational action by monopolists not justifiable in practice

The practical results of the widespread existence of collective bargaining may be more harmful than this discussion has suggested. For convenience and simplicity we have made here certain assumptions in regard to rational action on the part of combinations which cannot be justified in practice. The truth is that only the vaguest guesses as to the long-run elasticity of demand for products are possible in the actual economic world; and we find, as a result, that bilateral monopoly creates "indeterminateness" of wage rates in another sense—through causing the price- and wage-fixing mechanism to lose its sensitiveness. There arises a process of higgling between large and clumsy units in which the forces determining the settlement have only a remote connection with the interests of those members of the community who will be affected by the result. So undefinable are the forces which in such circumstances actually bring about the result that the adjective "indeterminate" well fits the case. Within the complex of factors determining price there are none which are sufficiently constant to be honored with the name of "cause." It often appears to the writer that the continued appearance of industrial depression in Great Britain is primarily due to the widespread existence of

---

[45]It is deplorable that this term has become so closely associated in the press with quota schemes and price-fixing cartels. Unfortunately, the stress is nearly always on "ration" not "rational."

monopolistic bodies on both sides which (quite apart from their having caused equipment and labor to remain idle by policies aiming at "not spoiling the market") have destroyed the sensitiveness of the price and particularly the wage system.

## Exploitation of the consumer hits the working class most heavily

The above analysis has sought to show that the ultimate gains of trade unions as well as monopolies of capital are obtained either by the "exploitation" of the consumer or the exclusion of competitors (although in the latter case, of course, the consumer also loses). In regard to gains at the consumers' expense, the effect upon distribution will depend upon the extent to which the owners of the different factors of production are the final consumers of the product concerned. In fact, we find that the greater part of the demand for consumers' goods is exercised by relatively poor people, and most of the commodities in whose manufacture the working class are employed are consumed by themselves as a class. This is a question of fact which has often been commented on.[46] Hence, apparent gains by workers at the expense of the consumer are likely, in general, to cause a more than proportionate real loss to them. If trade unions had, and exercised, the power to break down capitalists' monopolies they would benefit the workers of the community as consumers, but in practice their effect is to bolster up the capitalists' exclusiveness and to erect a dike (against potential competition) covering an even larger area.

## Trade unions are the wrong institution for attempting to improve distribution

Workers' combinations are impotent to secure a redistribution of the product of industry in favor of the relatively poor. Such a result cannot be achieved by interference with the value mechanism. Economists are all clearly conscious of the desirability of a more equal distribution of wealth; indeed, they base their case for it upon the firm foundation that it will lead to a maximization of economic welfare, and not upon abstractions

[46] E.g., cf. Pigou, *Economics of Welfare,* 2nd ed., pp. 646–48.

such as "natural right" or "justice." There are means of achieving greater equality that will still allow the value mechanism to function freely. It can be achieved by the thoughtful modification of economic institutions. But the consideration of this point lies outside the scope of this essay.

*The "legitimate" functions of trade unionism are perhaps concerned with other matters than wage rates*

The rate of wages which is best for the workers as a whole is that which is determined in the free market. The main useful function of collective bargaining may perhaps be negotiating about those things which, unlike prices or rates of wages, are *not* adequately determined by the market process. For example, hours of work and conditions of work are things that intimately concern workmen and are best decided collectively. They are a social matter, and ought, if possible, to express the will of the majority. "The *employer*" is concerned not so much with wages, hours, or conditions of work as with labor costs. Once it is recognized that shorter hours, or extra workshop comforts that cost money and do not add to efficiency, tend, in the absence of monopoly, to reduce wages, collective bargaining becomes an excellent thing. So long as one of the factors making up total labor costs is allowed to vary in harmony with economic change the value mechanism in society can continue to work. One cost factor at least must be a variable, and it is desirable that it should be the one which is most sensitive to change and therefore the most reliable index to guide human effort. That condition is satisfied by the rate of wages.

# III. 45 Years After: Who Exploits Whom?

## Introduction

### *Economic analysis of collective bargaining*

In parts 1 and 2, I showed why *attempts* to transfer income as a whole from rich to poor "by interference with the value mechanism," i.e., through the determination of the price of labor under duress,[1] must fail; and why such attempts must, indeed, harm the community (a) as consumers, (b) as sellers of efforts and skills, and (c) as investors. My main task in part 3, will be to demonstrate how, after consideration of history and discussion since 1930, these conclusions have been strengthened.

In parts 1 and 2, I suggested also that what is now (since about the middle 1950s) called "wage-push" was responsible for apparent depression. This phenomenon, I shall argue, is even more far-reaching today—the overwhelming cause of continuously threatened depression. And I try to show further how it is responsible for political recourse to three crude correctives: first, to spasmodic, mainly unanticipated, inflation; second, (when, later on, widespread expectations of rising prices have been aroused), to spasmodic, accelerating inflation; and third, to wage and price controls.

### *"Conceptual confusion" of classical and contemporary economists*

For academic economists, perhaps the most remarkable aspect emerging from parts 1 and 2 is the weakness of the

---

[1] I use "duress" in the same sense as the more common term "coercion."

arguments employed by sophisticated thinkers on the nature and consequences of trade-union practices. Nineteenth-century economists of impressive learning and formidable intellect, when confronted with the practice of wage bargaining, lapsed into conceptual confusion. Men like J. S. Mill, W. S. Jevons, F. Y. Edgeworth, and even the great Alfred Marshall became woolly when they had to consider the implications of strike power. They all then somehow inhibited consideration of the really central questions.

The importance of this phenomenon[2] lies in the similar weakness in academic circles in 1975. Many economists still seem unwilling to face the disconcerting reality that the strike-threat system, one of the most powerful institutions of the contemporary world, is demonstrably incapable of achieving the redistribution of income from rich to poor that is almost universally claimed as its chief raison d'être. Few draw attention to the truth that the union system as operated in this age must have enormously reduced the ability of modern society to provide for the material (and hence nonmaterial) well-being of the people. Nor are many prepared to show that the system is, for additional reasons, powerfully *regressive,* tending to burden the poor more than in proportion to their poverty. Economists are today widely conceding that "wage-push" has been overwhelmingly responsible for inflation. Yet union pressures on wage rates tend to be described, not very logically, as a "cause" of inflation, without explicit reference to the political expediency that is the crucial link in the chain of causation.[3]

## Economists' attitude to the significance of strikes

In other writings I have suggested two chief explanations for the pre-1930 economists' unsatisfactory treatment of the wages problem.

    (a) The economists' "virtues—warmth of heart, humanity, sheer kindness" have handicapped them.

[2] I have written on it in several works since the first edition of this present book: *Economists and the Public,* (London: Jonathan Cape, 1936); *Politically Impossible...?* (London: Institute of Economic Affairs, Hobart Paperbacks, 1972); *The Strike-Threat System* (New Rochelle: Arlington House, 1973).

[3] I return to this important aspect of "collective bargaining" in pp. 107–8, 110–13, 115, 125.

"Like their fellow intellectuals whom they have influenced, their sympathies have all too often ruled their minds. Stigler has charged that Marshall's great work was vitiated for this reason. I have charged that Adam Smith (whom I venerate) initiated a tradition of woolly thinking on the subject because he allowed his deep sympathy for the workers inappropriately to colour his judgement."[4]

(b) The economists have "tried to be influential in the easiest way, obscuring their political assumptions, and thereby destroying scientific unanimity, especially on the subject of labour's share in income."[5] This "fight for a hearing," as I called the process in 1936,[6] has often been disinterested.[7]

### Irrelevance of "macroeconomic formalism"

During the last two decades there has been a movement among a group of economists who call themselves "neo-Keynesians" (although nothing that Keynes said would give any support to the developments to be discussed here) to put forward a type of analysis which suggests that profits can be confiscated without harm to general living standards. Working within what may be termed "conceptually nonrigorous macroeconomics," they disparage the market process.[8] The disparagement is not the conclusion of a careful analysis. Professor L. M. Lachmann has summarized a principal weakness of their "macroeconomic formalism," which is how he describes their treatment of abstract entities as if they were real. They envisage, he says, an abstract model of society in which "there is no room for entrepreneurs.... Differences of preferences and divergencies of expectations do not matter." And when expectations must somehow be incorporated into the model, the complexities are evaded "by assuming that everybody expects the future to be like the past."

[4] *The Strike-Threat System*, p. 285.
[5] Ibid., p. 285.
[6] *Economists and the Public*, chap. 10.
[7] *The Strike-Threat System*, p. 285.
[8] Aspects of this debate are discussed in Mark Blaug, *The Cambridge Revolution* (London: IEA, Hobart Paperbacks, 1974).

I suggest that any such approach to the study of functioning society excludes, through its assumptions, fruitful consideration of almost every true economic problem,[9] not least the theory of collective bargaining and the determination of incomes.

"Macroeconomic formalism" has nothing to contribute to, and merely diverts attention from, the basic issues relevant to income distribution.

## Internal Administrative Influences on Wage Rates and Profits

*The alleged "separation of ownership and control" in an epoch of corporations*

Another consideration which did not arise in 1930 is concerned with what has become known as "the separation of ownership and control." In their critique of the market process and the loss-avoidance, profit-seeking incentives which activate it, some economists have argued that little or no meaning can be accorded to theoretical studies of income distribution based on the assumption that managements are engaged in profit-maximization for investors' benefit. It is held that the executives we call "management"—the decision-makers *within* a corporation, responsible to shareholders and authorized to make entrepreneurial and saving ("plow-back") decisions— tend to maximize their own utility rather than avoid losses and seek profits for the shareholders and others who provide assets and risk capital. "Though these pronouncements lack empirically refutable content," writes Professor Armen Alchian, "their emotional impact rivals that of a national anthem."[10]

---

[9]Cf. L. M. Lachmann's important essay, *Macro-economic Thinking and the Market Economy* (London: IEA, Hobart Paperbacks, 1973), from which the passages quoted have been taken, pp. 18 and 23.

[10]"Corporation Management and Property Rights," in E. G. Furubotn and S. Pejovich, eds., *The Economics of Property Rights* (Cambridge, Mass.: Ballinger, 1974), p. 134. Alchian quotes the following economists who have put forward these views of entrepreneurship in practice: R. J. Larner, P. A. Samuelson, A. Berle and G. Means, and C. Kaysen.

There is, I admit, a very strong case indeed for bringing such possibilities into economic analysis. The content of the property rights conferred on corporation management (as well as on politicians and government officials) requires explicit and critical examination. But this question is of little direct relevance to the specific problems of income determination. My study of industry[11] suggests that the abuses arise primarily only where "profits" are constrained by "controls" (as in "regulated" public utilities, in "not-for-profit" undertakings, in state-owned corporations or in large state-engineered mergers such as British Leyland). In other cases, unless competition is weak, the shareholders' interests cannot persistently be ignored, even although the shareholders may be regarded (as it has been argued) not as true owners of the undertaking but merely as lenders to it of risk capital.[12]

Where managements may *seem* to line their own pockets, they may usually be regarded as operating within the terms of a contract which purposely allows them a very flexible discretion. On this view, the luxurious offices, plush carpets, pretty secretaries, generous leave, travel and expense accounts, and the other perquisites described as illustrations of managements' independent property rights, may be regarded most realistically as fringe benefits—nonpecuniary inducements to retain or attract executive personnel of the appropriate calibre—especially in conditions of a high marginal rate of tax on salaries, even higher in Britain than in the United States or Europe. And like fringe benefits for wage-paid employees, they are usually tax-exempt (pp, 101–2). Generous executive pensions are expressly authorized in board meetings, while benefits such as stock options and managerial commissions are, in economic essence, contractual arrangements for participating in profits, whether or not the technical accounting methods present them as a share in profits or as costs which reduce profits. But when managements do abuse their trust, they acquire part of the profits. Hence their incentive to maximize profits and minimize

[11][Professor Hutt was Professor of Commerce at the University of Cape Town from 1931 to 1965 and made a close study of business administration.—ED.]

[12]A fuller discussion of these issues is in Brian Hindley, *Industrial Mergers and Public Policy* (London: IEA, Hobart Paperbacks, 1970).

losses remains, even although we can expect unauthorized appropriations of profits to be disguised as costs.

The major danger arising from managerial independence appears not to be the possible dishonesty of top executives but their biased judgment on "plow-back." "Empire building" by ambitious managements may, at times, have been a reality. But the growth of a firm inspired solely by the search for the personal prestige of managers could not long continue if increased dividends failed to follow "plow-back." No evidence presented by economists who condemn entrepreneurial incentives and action in practice has shown, for instance, that decisions about large acquisitions of fixed plant are not typically made with the aim of achieving the optimal scale of the investment in terms of forecast (i.e., probable) yields. Complete integrity (as distinct from erroneous judgment) is nearly always assured unless there is fraudulent collusion among board members. Hence the consequences of strike-threat duress upon the composition of the assets stock and the willingness of investors to provide risk capital are not removed by "the separation of ownership and control."

*The "jolt theory" is not valid*

An equally hollow notion is what is known as the "jolt theory."[13] The contention is that costs imposed by coercion give managements such a jolt that they are goaded into becoming more efficient. But if incentives to substitute lower-cost methods of producing and marketing could be stimulated in that way, we should find industrialists lobbying for, say, increased corporation taxes, not for subsidies or protective tariffs.

This criticism of the "jolt theory" does not deny, of course, that managements react to costs imposed by coercion in the same sort of way as they do to all other changes in value. They will resort to labor-economizing arrangements or acquire labor-saving machinery in their search for a lower-cost solution. But that cannot be accepted as "greater efficiency."[14]

[13]The theory was given respectability by Walker, Marshall, Pigou, and (cautiously) by Bowley.
[14]Cf. *The Strike-Threat System,* pp. 157–159.

## *The effect of the strike-threat process on workers' morale*

Among the detriments caused by the strike-threat system, the importance of which may conceivably be very large indeed, is the effect of the shadow it casts upon the efficiency of cooperation within the firm. The harmful consequences involve more than reduction of the outputs of goods or services that contribute to the material well-being of the people. The "quality of life" among the employed must also be adversely affected. Because the strike is a kind of warfare, it comes to be regarded as essential tactics for the unions to create and keep alive the war spirit—mistrust and suspicion of "the enemy": "the bosses"—managements or investors.

To insist that this war spirit must have had a deplorable effect upon the workers' morale in their place of employment is almost to emphasize the obvious. Engineered hostility to "the bosses" frustrates attempts to achieve a friendly atmosphere. There are writers on personnel management who speak about the aim of creating one big happy family or a club-like environment within a large enterprise. But it is condescension to assume that the harmony, mutual respect, and pride of membership within a well-administered university[15] cannot be duplicated within the disciplined hierarchy of a firm.

## *The rationale of market-caused pay differentials*

Under a system of industry in which commands must be communicated through instructions passed down the lines of authority (from top executives to overseers, foremen, and personnel), positive efforts to achieve a spirit of cooperation and understanding need no apology whatever the social or political system, capitalist or communist. The term "paternalism" is not a significant description of such efforts. In every cooperative venture the exercise of personal authority is inevitable, even when the leadership requires nothing more than a coordinating command like "pull" to a group combining to move a

---

[15]The traditional good relations within a university, of course, can be sabotaged through a borrowing of strike-threat and shop-steward techniques, as has happened in British and other universities in the past decade. Parts of this development are discussed in A. T. Peacock and A. J. Culyer, *Economic Aspects of Student Unrest,* Occasional Paper 26, IEA, 1969.

heavy weight. But proved (as distinct from latent) ability to manage, that is, to predict and act through command at different levels in the administrative pyramid, is scarce. The more severe the scarcity is judged to be, the higher the remuneration that will be offered. Hence there is normally a wide range of earnings in the firm or plant. But this need not lead to friction unless the very human trait of envy is deliberately inflated.

Nevertheless, it is sometimes argued by economists critical of the determination of wage rates in the market that wage-rate differences within a firm must inevitably give rise to friction. The suggestion is that enforced equality within a firm can improve productive performance through permitting a more effective "team spirit." Yet wide differences in remuneration for members of a team in professional sport or entertainment in Britain and other Western countries suggest no empirical confirmation to such notions. Why is industry singled out?

Differences of remuneration due to varying degrees of efficiency as estimated by managements, it has been argued, destroy the incentive for employees with special knowledge and skill to impart their expertise to the less skilled or the unskilled. Hence, the theory says, enforced uniformity of remuneration can raise the profits of a firm. If that were so, managements would have come to perceive it and have voluntarily abolished differentials. It is difficult to see why they should have waited for union coercion to raise their profits.

In reality, market-caused differentials work in the opposite direction. The literature of management, which reflects recorded experience, certainly emphasizes the continuous training process required in most businesses to meet equally continuous changes in machinery and tools, as well as in consumer preferences. But the process of investment in human capital through training requires, inter alia, incentives for those who wish to improve their value as employees.[16] In most circumstances, a narrowing of market-determined wage differentials under pressure would weaken the motive for self-

[16]It also needs incentives for the firm to invest in training. In the extreme case it may require resort to a "lock-in" contract. But in the absence of fears of strike-threat coercion, managements would most often feel confident of being able to outbid rivals for the services of the workers whose value has been raised through the firm's investment in "human capital."

improvement. The prospect of increased individual earnings is an effective carrot, especially for men (or women) with families. Hence, while it is undeniable that an experienced or skilled worker may be loath to impart his knowledge or skill to others, and that an employee who has subordinates may fear their competition, try to hold back their progress, and perhaps report falsely upon their cooperativeness and technical performance, these are such commonplace possibilities, not only in industry but in government, "nonprofit" activities, the Armed Services, and life generally, that every rationally organized personnel structure in business or elsewhere is designed with a view to minimizing the expected inefficiencies.

Again, the reason why the techniques of job evaluation and merit rating have been so widely adopted (in spite of an occasionally large degree of arbitrariness) is that managements have learned how important it is for good morale that remuneration shall vary in accordance with entrepreneurial judgments of the value of *individual* employees to the firm.

### Nonmarket Influences on Wages and Profits

*Attempts to exploit investors via the strike threat are normally self-defeating*

Curiously, the chief theoretical question is very simple. By insisting that union pressures cannot redistribute *income* from the suppliers of assets as a whole to the suppliers of labor as a whole, I do not imply that the strike threat cannot be used to seize *property*. This notion is hardly new. Being a coercive device, it can be used, as Professor Ludwig von Mises emphasized as long ago as 1958, as the "gun under the table."[17] Once investment has been made in fixed, nonversatile (i.e, specific) assets, the threat to disrupt the productive process through the concerted withdrawal of labor can be used to confiscate a part of the value of the investment: as much as is

[17]L. von Mises used this telling phrase in addressing the Princeton meeting of the Mont Pelerin Society in 1958. In his *Human Action,* 1st ed., 1949, p. 773, he used the phrase, "what is euphemistically called 'collective bargaining'...is bargaining at the point of a gun."

thought expedient. It can be said that, in every successful use of the strike threat against a corporation, the fall in the total value of its shares following the wage "agreement" represents in part the capital value of the property transferred.[18] Assuming that there is (a) no "joint monopoly" (pp. 67–72), and (b) full replacement of depreciation and sales of output,[19] investors' income will fall by the same amount as that by which the workers' income has increased.

But that is not all. An enormous volume of *potential* investment will be scared away from kinds of production in which such property seizures are predictable. Marginal prospective yields to new investment in enterprises and projects vulnerable to strikes or strike threats, on the one hand, and those not so vulnerable, on the other, will thus still tend to equality. This proposition is central to the analysis and is elaborated on pp. 94–98, 103, 123.

*Strike threat: some ethical considerations*

Instead of "property *transferred*" the words "property *stolen* through union duress" could have been used. But they might have sounded emotive. Even so, it must be recognized that a threatened strike is a form of private coercion. And although no one could question the possibility of strike-threat power being used for good objectives, or objectives which some people would regard as good,[20] so can other methods of intimidation. The question is whether private duress should be tolerated more when it takes the form of a threat to withhold labor disruptively. If it should, its difference in this respect from blackmail, hijacking, kidnapping, the use of hostages,

---

[18]The skeptical reader will find a rigorous proof of this proposition in *The Strike-Threat System,* pp. 135–36. Briefly, if the total value of a corporation's shares falls by 25 percent following capitulation to a strike or strike threat (because its predicted earning power has been reduced in that proportion), the union members may be regarded as having seized one-quarter of its capital. (Ibid., p. 136.)

[19]This assumption must, of course, usually imply that demand for the output is highly inelastic or increasing.

[20]For example, to take from people felt to have "too much" for the benefit of those with "too little."

and other methods of extortion must be made clear.[21] It is investors (shareholders) who finance the provision at risk of

(a) fixed assets (labor's tools),
(b) the materials used in production,
(c) managerial services, and
(d) investment in labor's inputs.

In doing so, investors enormously *magnify* the yield to human effort. It could be held, therefore, that in every case in which investors are harmed because they had not expected a seizure of part of their property, the exploitation is doubly reprehensible.

There is another, curiously neglected, ethical aspect. As in other warfare, victory in a strike is to the strong, not the just; and often noncombatants suffer most.[22] It is remarkable that humanitarians have not striven to rescue the wage-determination process from such warfare.

### The market (i.e., social) determination of wage rates is the sole peaceful method

The only imaginable alternative to the veiled assault of the strike-threat system is the social (i.e., market) determination of labor's remuneration. It can, I argue, be achieved only by protecting the market process

(i) from force exerted on behalf of private interests *through* government, or
(ii) from private duress and collusion *tolerated* by government.

If the value of the product that workers sell—their contribution to work in progress—is to be ascertained peacefully, the free market provides the only solution.

It may of course be objected that, although wage rates are peacefully arrived at in this way, there can be no assumption that the resulting income distribution must necessarily be

---

[21]On the day this was written, the organized firemen of Montreal succeeded in imposing a permanent burden on local taxpayers in the form of higher wages because serious fire damage was being caused to property while the bargaining was in progress. Comparable cases have occurred in Britain in recent years, when old people have suffered most in so-called "public service" strikes through their inability to get fuel or other essentials.

[22]Below, p. 103.

"just." Then what *principles* of distributive justice are envisaged? Where have they been objectively and unequivocally enunciated? It is true that monopsonistic power of a single seller or oligopsonistic power of a handful of sellers may, theoretically, be abused for investors' advantage; market values will not then be "free-market values." But if, through such abuse, some managers can (on behalf of themselves or investors) exploit the workers, the defensible remedy should be sought through antiexploitation laws, not through private warfare.[23] But if the *free* market determination of the price of labor is alleged to leave an "unfair" division of the value of the product, it remains true that the influence of union coercion must be to aggravate, not mitigate, the injustice. For labor costs raised above the free-market value (whether by private coercion or state edict) have regressive consequences from every angle: not only does the strike-threat system formidably repress the flow of wages in total; it also exerts an *inegalitarian* influence upon its distribution.[24]

### There are no rigorously argued criteria for "justice" in redistributing incomes determined by the market

It has not, of course, been implied that the determination of individual incomes in accordance with the free-market value of (a) people's efforts and (b) the services of their property is necessarily "just," in the light of all conceivable ethical standards. But there have been no attempts at rigorous enunciation of alternative principles.

How can a "just" scale of relative remuneration for different kinds of work be formulated without a free market? The assertion that the rich have too much and the poor too little gives no clue to the proportions in which it is thought income should be divided, still less of any *rationale* for those proportions. From Jevons onwards, there were of course "welfare economists" who argued (as did my great teacher, Edwin Cannan) that any achievement of more equality of income raised the wealth of a nation because of the diminishing marginal

---

[23]The frequently used (and abused) term "exploitation" is seldom defined, even in the loosest way. It is defined in the appendix to this chapter.
[24]Pp. 96, 104–5, 122–23.

utility of income.[25] But they never intended that a government should seek to increase a country's wealth by successive income transfers until absolute income equality (and so maximum wealth) was achieved. The qualification of ceteris paribus (other things being equal) was always implicit. There was the question of incentives to be considered, for instance, as well as the problem of allocating men and assets in accordance with the people's preferences.

What the economists' teachings really came down to was that regressive influences were generally to be deplored and progressive influences to be welcomed. It was for that reason that Henry Simons[26] pointed to the superiority of income transfers over strikes as a method of trying to reduce inequalities. But theories about "welfare" based on the marginal utility of income were undermined when it came to be generally perceived that comparisons of utility between individuals had no meaning.

Economists then found themselves even further from any rational criteria for defining a defensible degree of redistribution. Some tried to surmount the difficulty by treating it as though it concerned aesthetics. But this device threw no light on the question how far, say, a program like progressive taxation combined with "reverse (negative) income tax" ought to go. Among economists who have recommended such income transfers, some have done so wholly on pragmatic grounds. For instance, in the opinion of some, "negative income tax" would have harmful effects on incentives, although they advocate it simply because it is regarded as less harmful than the alternative—costly administered social services in kind, with their even more damaging destruction of incentives, their demoralization of welfare recipients, and the concealed squandering of the capital that could multiply the wages flow. Such an ap-

[25]From which it seemed to follow that additional pounds in the hands of a pensioner would add more in "total utility" than in the hands of a plutocrat. Since Jevons, wrote Cannan, "it has been impossible...to rely much on the fact that a loaf is a loaf whether it is crumbled in the hands of a surfeited Dives or devoured by a starving Lazarus. The same loaf is of less use to Dives, and the modern economist must recognize the fact." (Edwin Cannan, *Theories of Production and Distribution,* 3rd ed. London: P. S. King, 1917), p. 396.

[26]"Some Reflections on Syndicalism," in *Economic Policy for a Free Society* (Chicago: University of Chicago Press, 1948), p. 128.

proach, however, hardly helps economists groping for principles.

*Ethically indefensible income transfers*

Although there seem no unambiguous *positive* principles, there are what might be called *negative* precepts. Income transfers must, I suggest, be socially harmful and hence ethically unacceptable if they are
  (i) from the industrious for the benefit of the indolent;
 (ii) from the provident for the benefit of the thriftless;
(iii) from the responsible for the benefit of the irresponsible;
(iv) from the competent for the benefit of the incompetent;
 (v) from the lucky for the benefit of the unlucky;[27] or
(vi) from the politically weak (generally minorities) for the
       benefit of the politically strong (generally majorities).
These principles condemn many or perhaps most transfers that occur through taxation and welfare benefits.

I have always been impressed, however, by one special case of the lucky, namely, he "who has chosen his parents wisely." There is a special advantage to people who have inherited capital, or a favorable home environment, or an expensive education, or good habits and manners, or a good disposition, or (through genetic factors) good minds, physiques, or looks. But is the advantage they enjoy "unjust"? There is an enormous advantage, pecuniary or otherwise, to a girl who is born beautiful of face and figure. Ought society to try to rectify such "injustices" by income transfers? There are no satisfying answers to these questions.

*Communally owned private capital as a solution*

Nevertheless there is a case for redistributing inherited property on wholly different grounds. Accumulated knowledge can be regarded as the common inheritance of mankind. On this proposition (ignoring the question of patents and copyrights),[28]

---

[27]Because insurance (commerical or collective) can cover the bad luck of being crippled, or blind, or deaf, etc.

[28]The leading economic authority on patents and copyrights is Professor Sir Arnold Plant, some of whose main papers on these subjects are collected in *Selected Economic Essays and Addresses* (London: Routledge and Kegan Paul for the IEA, 1974).

there appears to be no controversy. But much of that knowledge is embodied in the technical composition of the aggregate stock of assets, which may give some support to the point of view about to be explained.

Can it not be said, perhaps, that the business of living can be improved by *reducing* the luck element, just as, in games of skill, the reduction of the chance factor often raises the appeal of the game? It is not suggested that winners should be compelled to share their winnings with the losers but that *one* special inherited advantage can be reduced—namely, inherited capital. Part of the aggregate stock of capital can, perhaps, be gradually brought into common, "communal" ownership[29] without the change of rules creating feelings of gross injustice or destroying the incentives for socially beneficial entrepreneurship. The method is that of gradually accumulating a large capital fund, owned by the people, not by the government, and raised via inheritance taxes progressively graded according to the size of the inheritance received, and not according to the sum bequeathed. The essential difference is that the sum raised in this way, which should include the aggregate sum raised by any surviving progressive principle in income taxes, would be maintained intact (placed beyond the reach of governmental greed) and lent back to competitive industry, at the market rate of interest, for productive purposes.

Initially, the additional proceeds from the inheritance duties would have to be used to pay off the community's collectively owned *negative* capital, namely, the national debt. The gradual redemption of this debt would, of course, cumulatively lighten

[29]Professor Harold Demsetz, in a path-breaking article, "Towards a Theory of Property Rights," *American Economic Review,* 1967, p. 354, uses the term "communal" as distinct from "collective" for the category of ownership envisaged. He writes: "Communal ownership means that the community denies to the state or to individual citizens the right to interfere with any person's exercise of communally owned rights." On the other hand, "State ownership implies that the state may exclude anyone from the use of a right so long as the state follows accepted political procedures for determining who may not use state-owned property." Demsetz does not deal, however, with communal capital as we have here conceived of it. The nature of property is discussed by Sir Arnold Plant, *Selected Economic Essays,* who refers to the analysis of David Hume in 1751. The latest thought on property rights is to be found in the symposium edited by Furubotn and Pejovich, referred to above (footnote, p. 78).

the future weight of proportional taxation, the burden of which would fall in each successive year. Thereafter a communally owned fund of *positive* capital would accumulate. This fund could then be lent to entrepreneurs at whatever the market rate of interest happened to be. The earnings of the fund could first be applied to reduce still further the rate of proportional taxation, which, we can reasonably assume, would be substantially reduced when (apart from those paying estate duties) every income group had to pay the same rate of income tax. Eventually, there would be no income taxes left, all government costs being met wholly out of interest on the communal capital fund. At that point, continued accumulation of the fund would allow its excess earnings to be paid out to the people as dividends, rather like pensions, in proportion to each person's annual earnings from work *plus* property. This last provision would be needed to preserve the incentive to work and to save.

The main objection to the achievement of increased equality by such a method is that it would end the system which many opinion makers, as well as "radical political scientists" and "radical economists," believe is an expression of true democracy: the tradition under which politicians, with not disinterested generosity, try to offer majorities, or "swing" voting groups, more than their opponents—at the expense of minorities. On the other hand, it would weaken the objection that the free-market determination of prices and incomes is unjust in itself; and that could enormously improve the relations between owners who supply the assets that multiply the yield to work and "workers" who benefit from the multiplication.

### *Increased "labor productivity" in an industry does not necessarily justify higher wage rates in it*

It is common today in Britain and America to regard "increases in the productivity of labor" as a justification for forcing up wage rates in a firm, occupation, or industry. Now it is true that an improvement in the productivity of men and assets within a firm may frequently increase prospective yields from investment in it, including investment in labor's inputs.[30] But

[30]The owners of an enterprise "invest" in "inputs" such as raw materials,

the improved productivity may not raise the profitability of the whole industry, or of the whole occupation, only that of the economizing firm. The incentives for economizing may be loss-avoiding as well as profit-seeking. Hence an improvement in the productivity of an industry constitutes no reason why the remuneration of labor and the services of assets *in that industry* should necessarily rise. Ceteris paribus, it is improved productivity in *noncompeting* industries which creates additional demand for its output and thereby validates higher pay for its contribution.

### *"Labor productivity" is often a misnomer*

Excluding managerial ingenuity and acumen, it is doubtful whether human skills relevant to the goods and services which contribute to the· well-being of mankind have improved one iota since the beginning of the industrial age.[31] Today's typists are no more skilled than those of the 1890s. Techniques of typing have improved, and typewriters (i.e., capital assets) have improved, but not the operators. Yet the real earning power of the operators is very much higher. Again, the value of ordinary unskilled labor, providing mere "put and carry work," leaves the laborer of this generation affluent in comparison with the ordinary laborer of previous ages—say, 150 years ago in the early days of the Industrial Revolution.[32] But the workers' growing material well-being has not been a consequence of increasing efficiency on their own part, except to the extent that more plentiful nutrition, improved education, and a generally ameliorating environment (themselves consequences of rising *physical* well-being) have been present.

---

semifinished goods, fuels, money stocks and labor. Such "inputs" are embodied in work in progress and ultimately in final outputs of goods or services.

[31] Intensity of effort (in relation to time) has probably increased considerably, especially under payment by results or other incentive payment practices. But this does no more than offset, to some extent, a decline in hours worked.

[32] The growth in real incomes before and since the Industrial Revolution, and the reasons for it, are discussed by economists and economic historians in R. M. Hartwell et al., *The Long Debate on Poverty,* IEA Readings No. 9, 1973 (second edition 1974, with an essay by Professor Norman Gash on "The State of the Debate").

*Labor's earning power has increased* despite *the strike threat*

It has been thrift, entrepreneurial enterprise, and especially "the economizing-displacement process" that have been raising the earning power of labor and adding to the means for improving the material and moral well-being of the people. This achievement has been accomplished because these factors have been more than offsetting the impoverishing consequences of strike-threat power.

The offsetting factor to union-caused impoverishment has been chiefly what I like to call "the economizing-displacement process." Through this process, it has become possible to produce given outputs with fewer workers (the labor-economizing case), or with assets of reduced real value (the capital-economizing case).[33] Costs of production and marketing have been drastically reduced for the common advantage. Indeed, ever since the invention of the wheel, "the economizing-displacement process" has been releasing labor and other assets for the production of additional objects (either different objects, or additional supplies of the same kinds of outputs).[34] In so displacing labor and cheapening assets in one activity, this process has been continuously raising the real value of labor in other activities generally, that is, raising the real wage-rates at which "full employment" of labor as a whole can be achieved, as well as raising prospective and realized yields to noncompeting investment.[35]

Hence it is the consequential contribution to the source of demands for inputs and outputs in *noncompeting* spheres of production which is of primary importance in every case. Cheapened inputs and outputs in the industry to which the specialized economizing assets are provided raise real wage-rate offers in *other* industries, by augmenting demands for outputs in general.[36]

[33]Presumably because fewer workers are required to produce the assets.

[34]Unless demand for the product is judged to be highly elastic, in which event workers who would otherwise be "released" by the economy achieved will be able to provide additional inputs of the same kind.

[35]This is an implication of "Say's Law," discussed in *A Rehabilitation of Say's Law* (Athens, Ohio: Ohio State University Press, 1974).

[36]The most important attributes of the assets and managerial arrangements which secure these benefits seem to be specialization and largeness of scale of

The ability of given muscle power and given skills (innate or acquired) to command ever-growing real remuneration has been solely a consequence of the virtues of (a) thrift and (b) enterprise (invention, originality, imagination, and risk taking) in the very people against whom the strike-threat system is *ostensibly* aimed. The workers have, on the whole, been incomparably better remunerated in each succeeding decade, almost entirely because they have been the beneficiaries of

(i) "the propertied classes," whose providence has made available the means for rising productivity, namely, a continuous net accumulation of assets (materials, equipment, machinery, and the like) and training—investment in "human capital";

(ii) the explorers, discoverers, scientists, inventors, and innovators; and above all,

(iii) people in their entrepreneurial capacity.[37]

Yet the unions throughout the past 100–150 years have been attempting to despoil those who have accumulated and conserved the community's assets stock, determined what they have predicted to be the "assets mix" most likely to create income,[38] and responded to incentives to minimize the cost of the assets. And the cheapening of assets, particularly of fixed assets, has enormously benefited not only consumers indirectly, but also directly those who use the assets—the workers. That is why, as the twentieth century has progressed, in spite of the continuous tendency to impoverish the people through

---

operations both in industry and in marketing. In the United States misconceptions about the *rationale* of monopoly control and the nature of "exploitation" have seriously discouraged, but not suppressed, this source of material well-being for the people. Clumsily formulated "regulations" almost *invite* large corporations to exclude interlopers. (Carl E. Person, *How to Beat the System,* Paralegal Institute, New York, 1973.)

[37]Especially the managements to whom investors delegate entrepreneurial decision-making power (as well as an important part of the power to save—to plow back earnings or disinvest); and whose ingenuities are continuously devising lower-cost methods of coordinating human effort and skill with different "mixes" of assets. In so doing, managements are risking their stockholders' investment both in responding to predicted consumer preferences in the *form* of outputs and in economizing the means for replacing consumption and the net accumulation of assets. (But see pp. 80–82.)

[38]Including, of course, those who have *inherited* property in the stock.

strike-threat pressures in key activities the real values at which employment outlets as a whole have been available have been tending to rise steadily. I emphasize the words "in spite of."

*Appendix to Chapter 3: The Concept of "Exploitation"*[39]

Exploitation is "any action taken, whether or not through discernible private coercion (collusion) or governmental coercion, or whether through monopolistic or monopsonistic power, which, under a given availability of resources (including the stock of knowledge and skills), reduces the value of the property or income of another person or group of persons, or prevents that value from rising as rapidly as it otherwise would, *unless this effect is brought about through* (a) the dissolution of some monopolistic or monopsonistic privilege, or (b) the substitution of some cheaper method (labor-saving or capital-saving) of achieving any objective (including the production and marketing of any output); or (c) the expression of a change in consumers' preference; or (d) through taxation authorized by explicit legislation accepted as legitimate in any context."

My use of the term "exploit" in part 2 (i.e., in 1930) does not conform exactly to this definition in every context.

### Effects of Strike-Threat Power on Labor, Investors, and Consumers

*Investors will avoid assets vulnerable to strike threat*

Unfortunately, it is investment in exactly the type of specific assets we have been discussing that is most seriously restrained by the strike-threat system. When private coercion intended to take from investors becomes both lawful and "respectable," and hence generally expected, investment (the retention, replacement, or net accumulation of assets in different combinations) assumes forms that are relatively unexploitable. Entrepreneurs' forecasts of yields from the purchase of labor at

[39]This definition is quoted from the glossary in *A Rehabilitation of Say's Law*, p. 23.

wage-rate levels imposed by coercion reduce the magnitude of investment in such activities.[40]

In practice, the activities which will tend to be most avoided will be those in which the assets provided are the least versatile, and it is precisely the nonversatile assets driven away which would have multiplied the wages-flow most effectively had they been supplied.

It is huge investments in capital-economizing and labor-saving assets—factories with specialized machinery sunk into concrete—which, through making profitable large reductions in final prices, magnify most powerfully the yield to human effort. The benefits are secured mainly through increased demands for the outputs of noncompeting activities.

Investments in versatile (nonspecific, nonspecialized) assets are less vulnerable to strike-threat exploitation than those in nonversatile (i.e., specific) assets because some of the former can be diverted to other forms of production when labor costs are raised coercively. For instance, it is because such assets as printing machinery (particularly when specialized for newspaper production), coal-cutting machinery, and the equipment needed for aircraft production are so specific that the impoverishment of the people through the strike threat has the most burdensome and depressive incidence on the economy. Modern technologies are capable of enormously raising the wages-flow, especially through labor-economizing developments. It is because the benefits are experienced chiefly by workers and owners in noncompeting employments that this truth is seldom perceived (p. 92).

Hence the full potential benefits are withheld from society, especially when the provision of specific assets seems to serve, in itself, as an invitation to the unions to seize part of the savings embodied in them. The harm wrought, especially to lower-income groups, through *the composition* of the assets stock be-

[40]A commonplace example is that shoplifting in self-service stores limits investment in such forms of marketing. The predicted value of losses from pilferage becomes a cost of providing the economized retail services, just as the predicted value of seizures of property through the strike threat in a projected undertaking becomes a cost of production that curtails investment in it. In the shoplifting illustration, of course, the cost of surveillance, policing, and insurance may be decisive.

ing adapted to the risk of such depredations must be immense. As I have argued, fear of strikes is vastly more damaging to society than actual strikes. Because the alert investor who accurately assesses the risks and damage of strike threats is unexploitable, provision of the kinds of assets which could *most beneficially* improve people's material well-being ceases to be prospectively profitable.

### Strike threats exploit labor, not investors

Why "most beneficially"? Capital for any undertaking will be retained or supplied up to the point at which the *marginal* prospective yield to the investment is judged to be equated with the rate of interest, whether or not the undertaking is considered vulnerable to future strike-threat pressures. The probabilities of work stoppages after the undertaking begins to operate simply reduce the predictable fruits and so cause a contraction in the capital sum which entrepreneurs judge can be wisely risked. Hence, in the present era, *it is not primarily investors who are exploited through the successful use of the strike threat, but labor itself*—most seriously in other occupations, including many unionized occupations, as well as non-unionized employments. And the impoverishing consequences for consumers also bear disproportionately upon the poor.

Thus, if the price of leather is raised through collusive cartel action to exclude certain supplies, or through a strike-enforced rise in the price of labor, we can expect the profitable price of a pair of shoes to rise. (The circumstances in which this would not be true are of negligible importance.) More expensive footwear hits the relatively poor more severely than it hits the relatively affluent.

### Strike threats reduce labor's earning power

Moreover, even if we ignore *the form* assumed by assets, it should be clear that, in reducing the profitability of investment generally in the capital resources which are labor's tools, *organized labor has all along been repressing the earning power of labor*. Workers as a whole have been denied the cheapest as well as the most efficient complementary resources. Labor's advantage requires that the physical equipment of production (factory buildings, machinery, etc.) shall be cheap; but we find that it is in the manufacture of just such equipment that duress-imposed wage costs have curtailed profitable outputs most seriously. And we have to consider not merely the assets rendered more costly to the worker but those not provided at all. In any event, almost all assets which magnify the yield to effort and skill are made more costly than they could be; and the workers must shoulder the cost, as they would if they had to rent the assets.

It is one of the most puzzling phenomena of the twentieth century that political parties in Britain and elsewhere calling themselves "Labor parties" still defend or refrain from criticizing practices which have all along been repressing the total income of labor as well as creating inequalities of income.

*It is relatively easy to "exploit" men or assets by excluding them from a firm, occupation, or industry, but not easy by shutting them in*

An important aspect of attempts to achieve income redistribution through private coercion can now be generalized. Where the law does not forbid such conduct, it is usually not too difficult for parties in a competing relationship, acting in collusion, to exploit other competing, or potentially competing, parties by shutting *out* from an area, industry, occupation, or firm the resources they are capable of supplying. But it is extremely difficult for similar collusion to be used to exploit suppliers of complementary resources by shutting them *into* an area, industry, occupation, or firm.

The reasons are, first, that "shut-in" arrangements are conspicuous and hence eradicable under the laws which must always and everywhere constitute the framework of a free market; and secondly, because the complementary parties are, as producers, demanding one another's services.[41] It is obviously to the interests of both the owner-suppliers of assets and the worker-suppliers of labor that the inputs provided by the other shall flow continuously and be as plentiful as possi-

---

[41]"Shut-in arrangements" may merely be a method of exploiting competitors by denying them the right of access to the complementary resources.

ble. It is theoretically possible for managements, singly or in collusion, to exploit workers whom they fraudulently entice into acquiring specific skills. And managements may persuade workers to bind themselves to work exclusively for a particular firm or group through a contract secured by misrepresentation. Such possible abuses of market freedom are almost certainly negligible in practice; while if they do occur there are methods of tackling them other than via the strike-threat weapon.[42]

Moreover, "lock-in" contracts do not necessarily involve abuses. As in long-period contracts generally, both parties choose to take risks, knowing that changing circumstances will prove to be for the benefit of one party and the detriment of the other. In the absence of misrepresentation, then, no *injustice* can be charged. "Lock-in contracts" may, for instance, release an incentive for investment in "human capital," through binding employees who benefit from valuable "on-the-job" training to work for an agreed number of years at an agreed wage rate. Again, employees whose removal expenses are met by the firm they join may gain from a commitment to work for a minimum period.

These considerations alone suggest that what (since parts 1 and 2 were first published) has come to be termed "monopsonistic exploitation" can be of no more than negligible importance in the case of labor. Nevertheless it is expedient to examine the monopsony argument further.

## *Monopsonistic or oligopsonistic exploitation is unimportant and easily discernible*

The 1930 refutation (part 1) of the argument that strike power is needed by the workers to offset monopsonistic or oligopsonistic exploitation of workers by managements was reexamined in chapters 8 and 9 of *The Strike-Threat System*. The issue can be stated very briefly.

---

[42]An attempt to deal with this problem in more detail is in *The Strike-Threat System,* chap. 7, entitled " 'Exploitation'—by Shut-in or Shut-out." Briefly, both the "shut-in" and the "shut-out" are man-made barriers. The former prevents labor or assets from moving away from an area, occupation, or firm; the latter prevents labor or assets from moving in.

The conventional argument is that the abuse of monopsonistic power can force labor's remuneration below its "natural-scarcity" or "free-market" level. Theoretically, this is certainly possible. But there is a simple test of whether a wage rate conceded under strike-threat pressure is, or is not, offsetting an abuse of monopsonistic power by management or of oligopsonistic power by a small group of managements who dominate an industry. If a strike threat or a strike has had the effect of raising the wage rate in an occupation to the "free-market" or "natural-scarcity" level, no additional worker will be found who is prepared to accept this wage rate (or less).[43] If a union insists, in these circumstances, that would-be interlopers shall be refused access to the bargaining table to offer less than the wage rate conceded, it is admitting that, in its judgment, its forcing-up of the wage rate was *not* a countervailing of monopsonistic exploitation of employers, but a (presumably justified) exploitation of investors or others.[44]

The test of whether a wage rate is at or below the "free-market" or "natural-scarcity" level is whether any other people can be found who are prepared to perform identical work for that or a lower rate. As long as such people exist, the price of labor must be above the "free-market" level: and if a strike threat has enforced that price, it cannot be claimed that the effect had been to nullify attempted exploitation.[45] But I cannot conceive of any case in which, following a capitulation to strike-threat pressures, displaced workers or other interlopers would not be prepared, if free to do so, to accept less than the duress-imposed wage rate to keep their jobs in the firm or improve their earnings and prospects by moving to jobs in it.

### The exception of "joint monopoly"

I can imagine only two important exceptions to this rule. First, monopsonistic exploitation of labor can occur as an incidental (not necessarily unimportant) consequence of monopolistic exploitation of consumers. If managements of formerly

---

[43] *The Strike-Threat System,* p. 99.
[44] For example, displaced workers, or excluded workers, or consumers.
[45] For further explanation, ibid., pp. 98–99.

competing firms arrange to restrict their outputs, for example, they are reducing their demand for former inputs, including labor's inputs. Hence, especially to the extent to which the workers employed have specific skills, this action will reduce what had been the free-market value of the labor. Here the remedy obviously lies in antimonopoly (antitrust) action. Secondly, it is nearly always to the advantage of firms trying to exploit consumers that they enter into "joint monopoly" arrangements—what Americans today call "sweetheart contracts." Under such contracts, capital and labor can act in collusion and share in the spoils of exploitation.[46]

In practice, the initiative is most often from labor's side, although it seems at times to permit evasion of antitrust laws for the benefit of investors as well as employees. In the United States, for instance, the last steel contract has been said to resemble "a Viking blood oath between union and management to go to commit piracy on the high seas..."[47] There now exists, indeed, what might be not unfairly described as a legal steel cartel. Nevertheless, the "piracy" appears to have been wholly the consequence of strong union power, the solution having been accepted by steel industry managements with reluctance, as the only means of reducing the confiscation of investors' property. ("Joint monopoly" is discussed in parts 1 and 2, pp. 22, 67–72, and in *The Strike-Threat System,* pp. 50, 72–73, 110–11, 128.)

### "Bargaining power": a "vacuous concept"

It is unnecessary to develop further the discussion in part 1 of "labor's disadvantage in bargaining." Like the term "bargaining power," which Professors Alchian and Allen have

---

[46]A formal monopsony has for long existed for the purchase of African (black) labor for the South African mines. But in my judgment, the only *exploitation* of the Africans employed has been through legislative restraints (for the benefit of white labor) of their (the Africans') right to perform skilled or responsible work. This argument is developed and illustrated in *The Economics of the Colour Bar,* IEA, 1964.

[47]Nicholas von Hoffman (a syndicated columnist), quoted in H. C. Gordon, *Workers' Rights and Union Wrongs* (Nashville: United States Industrial Council, 1975), p. 8.

rightly called a "vacuous concept,"[48] it appears at times to have been used as a substitute for, rather than an aid to, economic analysis. Professor Fritz Machlup has exposed the futility of several apparent meanings which might be ascribed to "bargaining power,"[49] and chapter 5 of *The Strike-Threat System* attempts to unravel what could be intended by it in different contexts. The only significant uses of the term refer to either (a) a worker's alternative employment opportunities, or (b) a worker's vulnerability to monopsonistic exploitation. But the words "bargaining power" are an inappropriate description of the determinant of labor's pay in all conceivable circumstances.

*Fringe benefits may have been larger in the absence of the strike threat*

I have used the term "wage rate" for the price of labor (labor's inputs), though the relevant price of labor includes the value of fringe benefits, including nonpecuniary benefits. In the absence of strike fears, such benefits would probably have formed a larger proportion of labor costs; for, under freedom in the market, managements would have been likely to regard "the fringes" as conducive to good morale and very effective competitive inducements.

On the other hand, during negotiations conducted under the shadow of strike duress, managements often seem to find it profitable to make concessions in the form of improvements in "paid holidays," pensions, "severance pay," etc., as the cheapest way of allowing the negotiating union officials to claim substantial gains for their members.[50] In those circumstances the nonpecuniary element in the compensation of labor is likely to take a form less beneficial (i.e., less preferred by the workers) than would have resulted under nonstrike

[48]A. A. Alchian and W. R. Allen, *University Economics,* 3rd ed. (Paperback), Wadsworth/Prentice Hall International Editions, 1974, p. 446.

[49]F. Machlup, *The Political Economy of Monopoly, pp. 333–58.*

[50]This consideration is strengthened through the illusion that fringe benefits are "employers' contributions." But they are not a net addition to labor's (or management's) remuneration. They are simply one form in which remuneration is received.

bargaining. In practice, fringe benefits won under strike duress are, indeed, in the United States frequently referred to rather contemptuously as "icing on the cake" or "gravy on the meat." On the other hand, they have the advantage of being generally tax-exempt, which is of some importance in the higher-paid grades. But when fringe benefits contribute to a substantial proportion of labor costs, the effect may be to make overtime preferable (from both the union members' and the investors' viewpoint) to the early reabsorption of laid-off workers during recovery from recession.

### The significance of the strike threat in "public" services

Apologists for the use of strike power who contend that the purpose is to offset "oppression" by managements, to counterbalance exploitation for the benefit of avaricious investors, find it difficult to extend the argument to cover strikes of government employees. It is not so easy to allege monopsonistic exploitation of employees by avaricious, undertaxed taxpayers.

Rigorous analysis of the defensibility of such strikes, often described as "against the public,"[51] seems to expose the absurdity of the whole system. When workers in the "private" sector are allowed to exploit consumers, including public servants whose remuneration is not indexed, it seems obviously indefensible to deny government employees the right to use the same methods to force up *their* remuneration. If they do not, they may "lag seriously behind" in what is truly a free-for-all.[52] A rational public servants' organization could, however, take advantage of the possibility (p. 84) that strikes *could* be used for rightful purposes. If a public servants' association threatened a general strike in the "public" sector unless the government legislated to outlaw strikes in the "private" sector, they could bring about one of the most beneficial reforms of all time. But, as I have argued (p. 84), the

---

[51]In a real sense *all* strikes are "against the public."

[52]Such arguments have been used by British civil servants, local government officials, teachers, and workers in nationalized industries generally, with railwaymen the most recent example.

strike threat is in itself an indefensible weapon even when used for good purposes. We can hardly advocate a strike to end strikes, a war to end wars.

*The costs of strikes often fall most heavily on nonparties to a dispute, but the continuing effects of costs imposed by strike threat are far more burdensome*

One of the most frequent arguments in criticism of modern trade unionism is that the direct losses suffered during the course of strikes do not fall mainly upon the strikers and the specific investors whose assets are rendered temporarily idle. Damage to consumers of the product *plus* the temporary adverse consequences for investors and workers in *other* pursuits often constitute a much heavier burden. Yet such kinds of damage, however indefensible and burdensome, are minor in relation to the *continuing* burden due to labor being priced above its free-market value. Moreover, social detriment for this reason originates most often where there are no strikes to be blamed because managements capitulate to the unions during "peaceful" negotiations. The greatest harm of all is wrought through effects on the composition of the assets stock, and the consequential allocation of the labor force. As we have seen (pp. 94–97), investors avoid supplying such assets as they judge will render them vulnerable to strike-threat exploitation. That is mainly why I have insisted that *fear* of strikes is vastly more damaging to society than strikes themselves.

### The effect on thrift

Among the adverse consequences, we should perhaps mention the discouragement of provision for the future. It is difficult, of course, to assess how far the system has reacted adversely upon thrift—the general accumulation of additional assets. It may conceivably be that the less affluent the people of a country, the bigger the relative sacrifices of current final satisfactions they will make for the benefit of their children, or of themselves in retirement. But it is the composition, as distinct from the magnitude, of additions to or replacement of the assets stock that is adversely affected.

*The regressive consequences of strike-threat pressures*

The broad conclusion, so far, is that labor costs imposed by coercion on a firm, occupation, or industry do not primarily "exploit" the providers of assets but

(a) laid-off workers, or
(b) those who would otherwise have entered that firm or industry, i.e., had the "rate for the job" not excluded them from access to the bargaining table, or
(c) the whole community as consumers.

When the cost of labor's inputs is forced up in any occupation, ceteris paribus, the magnitude of profitable outputs will decline and curtail employment possibilities in it, while the laid-off workers will be forced into unemployment or "suboptimal" employments. In that event, the resources previously used to replace the assets the displaced workers had been using will, in turn, also be diverted to less productive, "suboptimal" activities. Alternatively, the rate of growth of the occupation will be slowed down and potential workers (juveniles or those in inferior occupations) who could have improved their earnings and prospects by finding a career in it, will have lost their opportunities. Finally, the whole community (i) as investors *plus* workers in other activities (demands for whose inputs are harmed by the general impoverishment), and (ii) as consumers, will be burdened regressively. For, ceteris paribus, the real values of curtailed outputs must rise, and the poorer consumers suffer from the rise more than proportionately. The unions cling to their traditional policy of seizing periodical wage-rate increases for members who can retain their jobs, while typically overlooking the incidence of the burden on others. This has been, for instance, a feature of recent wage "awards" to British power workers. The depressive incidence on all power-consuming producers is virtually unrecognized.

The strike-threat burden would be mitigated (not lifted) if unions were forced to share strike-threat gains with workers laid off, so that members losing their jobs were *fully* compensated, their incomes being brought into equivalence with the boosted earnings of workers who retain their jobs. As things are, laid-off workers typically receive only unemployment benefit.[53] The virtue of such a sharing of the spoils would be that it reduced the incentives for exploitation.

For reasons emphasized in pp. 94–98, the spoils of private coercion are seldom achieved at the expense of investors in the aggregate, whose detriment is normally in rough proportion to the shrinkage or constraint of real income as a whole. *Hence, the inegalitarian consequences of strike-threat pressures are flagrant from whatever angle the subject is approached.*

### Strike-Threat Power and Inflation

*Is "wage-push" to blame for inflation?*

The extent to which the material and moral well-being of the poorer people of union-dominated countries has been damaged through the strike-threat system would be difficult to estimate *statistically.*[54] But bearing in mind

  (i) the wage-multiplying power of nonversatile and so exploitable assets which are rendered more unprofitable or less profitable by the system, and
  (ii) the general regressiveness we have been discussing,
the harm wrought must have been enormous.

It is puzzling that observers in Britain have so far failed to perceive the inequalities, inequities, insecurity, and poverty resulting from the strike-threat system. But there has been a remarkable and growing tendency of recent years to blame the "wage-push" activities of the unions for chronic and accelerating inflation. The justification for this view can be examined initially by considering contemporary policy in Britain and the United States.

*Strike-threat pressures do not cause inflation directly, but are responsible for its political expediency*

If full employment had been sought, not via the crude reduction of real wage rates by inflation (i.e., the attempted forcing-

---

[53] *Theory of Idle Resources* (London: Jonathan Cape, 1939), pp. 134–35.

[54] I do not know of any attempt at such an estimate. Statisticians have been able to measure with some accuracy the degree to which, during eras in which

up of final prices generally relative to labor costs) but via action to increase the prospective real wages-flow by reducing the price of labor (money wage rates) to market-clearing levels, an immediate burst of prosperity would have been experienced. *Selective* reductions of some money wage rates, that is, of those which had been pushed too high to be consistent with employment for all the workers originally employed and were therefore repressing the economy as a whole, would have engendered an early rise in the average *money* wage rate[55] (assuming the absence of deliberate deflation), and of course an even larger rise in the average *real* wage rate. If such a policy is "politically impossible," as Keynes argued in the 1930s and as Keynesians still argue, that must be because opinion makers do not understand the implications. But the purpose at this stage is simply to discern and explain the causes of inflation.

Although unions are not *directly* to blame for inflation by pushing up wage costs, they cannot escape responsibility for wage-push pressures which create widespread prospective or actual unemployment of workers and for resisting the steps required to attain noninflationary prosperity in those circumstances. We have to recognize that, since the Second World War, the governments of Britain and the United States (as well as of other countries), through acquiescing in the use of strike-threat power, while accepting responsibility for "full employment," have unwittingly but irrevocably committed themselves

---

strikes and strike-threat power have been growing, the distribution of the aggregate product of industry has been changing in favor of "labor" and against "capital," or vice versa. Many independent investigations of this kind have been made in the United States. The evidence, summarized in chapter 16 of *The Strike-Threat System,* indicates that there has been no discernible change in the *proportion* between the remuneration of property and of effort and skill. It is the measurable consequences upon the size of the cake to be divided which would be so difficult to estimate. Such studies suggest that union pressures have failed to transfer income beneficially from property owners to workers, but have simply changed the composition of the assets stock and complementary labor skills disadvantageously to all. [The relative significance of the *share* of the total product going to labor and capital as a whole and the *price* of labor or capital, i.e., the share going to each worker or owner, is discussed in *The Cambridge Revolution,* where Professor Blaug contrasts the orthodox neoclassical tradition, which analyzes factor pricing, with the Cambridge School and its "obsessive preoccupation with distributive shares."—ED.]

[55]For this to be *necessarily* true the zero earnings of the unemployed would have to be reckoned in the average.

to inflation. This is because submitting to depression, and refraining from action to restrain labor-pricing practices that cause it, are judged *by the politicians* to lose more votes than does resort to inflation.

But in no other sense can it be charged that union pressures to fix wage rates under duress "cause" inflation. For if governments refrained from inflation, and some costs and output prices were raised by private coercion or government edict, either other costs and prices would be forced down and the employment of men and assets channeled into less productive activities, or the burden of temporarily idled or misallocated resources would be aggravated through a cumulative decline of real income. The latter would occur owing to a general failure of society to adjust costs and prices sufficiently rapidly to the initial impoverishment. What impositions by coercion on the market can always be blamed for is, then, that they impoverish, while each act of impoverishment exterminates a source of demands for other goods or services. As they operate today, the unions tend to repress income generally (and the wages component of income more or less proportionally) to below the otherwise attainable level, that is, the level which the stock of assets (of any given composition), entrepreneurial and scientific ingenuities, the available sources of muscular and mental effort, current knowledge and skills, and incentives for acquiring and communicating knowledge and skills *could* be providing.

*Strike-threat impoverishment does not necessarily cause cumulatively worsening unemployment and recession*

The proposition is that unemployment of men and assets (and hence the political expediency of inflation) is not *necessarily* caused by strike-threat impoverishment. An economy can adjust itself when the impoverishment process occurs slowly, or when it happens to be countervailed by the "economizing-displacement" process of technological progress. Laid-off workers (or excluded potential workers in an industry) may gradually accept suboptimal kinds of work, in which event, over the years, the composition of the stock of assets will adapt itself to the situation.

An additional reason why depression need not follow if entrepreneurial and inventive ingenuities *plus* thrift are adding to, or improving, the machinery used by labor is that aggregate real output need not decline. Indeed, it may continue to grow even though its rate of growth is slowed down by strike-threat pressures.[56] It is when the impoverishment factor operates so rapidly and continuously that workers and the providers of assets find demands for their services declining, with prices no longer market-clearing, that prospective unemployment and recession cannot be staved off—except by cost and price reductions or by inflation to make profitable the employment of labor and capital that would be unprofitable without it.

### The nature of "wage-push"

The phenomenon that economists have come to call "wage-push," perhaps not always with a sufficiently rigorous perception of its essential attributes, describes the periodic attempts by unions generally to ensure that those of their members expected to keep their jobs when their real pay is forced up shall gain at least as much as members of other unions that follow the same policy. The British National Union of Railwaymen (NUR) in June 1975 extracted a 30 percent increase in wage rates largely, it seemed, because it did not see why it should fall behind the National Union of Mineworkers (NUM). And under inflation, because costs and prices rise year by year, incentives induced by envy or "comparability" cause each unionized occupation to rely on strike power to see that their real earnings keep pace with the rest, thus preventing past inflation from exerting all or most of its crude coordinative influence.[57] Union officials who fail to win increases as substantial as those achieved by other unions are apt to be regarded as incompetent. The upward pressures are justified, each union can claim, because comrades in other firms or industries are continuously benefiting or protecting themselves by similar

---

[56]Time preference being assumed to remain unchanged.

[57]Unanticipated inflation "crudely coordinates" economic activity in the sense that it increases the prospective yields to investment because labor costs lag behind the expected prices of output.

pressures. Wage-push comes to appear, therefore, as un-challengeably "legitimate" action to shelter the workers from the injustices of rising prices, while managements capitulate to union demands because they can rely on inflated money-spending power to validate the concessions. That is, it is expected that higher prices to offset higher wage rates will not cause such a fall in demand for the product as to lead to many jobs being lost.

Sometimes it is the rising money wage rates of workers in nonunion occupations (whose remuneration may merely be catching up under inflationary market pressures, *without* the coercion of wage-push) that ignites the natural human weakness to keep up with others. At other times, when craftsmen or skilled workers in the same industry are involved, the incentive is often to make sure that the real wage rates for the crafts shall rise at least proportionately to those of the unskilled.[58] But each raising of costs causes profitable outputs to contract and loss-minimizing prices to rise. Hence, a persistent upward pricing of labor in an important range of activities, with the prospective impoverishment offset continuously by inflation, is forced upon the community.

### *"Wage-push" and government*

It is the perpetual application of such pressures—the periodic, persistent, chronic use of the threat to disrupt—that constitutes wage-push. The politicians, sometimes with misgivings but often seeming to think "after the deluge," acquiesce. They react to the threatened contraction of aggregate "purchasing power" by increasing "money-spending power." And when the impoverishing pressures, and managerial capitulations, are encouraged by expectations of further inflation, everything tends to happen so rapidly that labor and other resources are thrown into idleness faster than the central bank is adding to effective "money-spending power." Political pressure upon the monetary authority to accelerate inflation then appears to be inescapable. Governments are generally unwilling to put the interests of pensioners and other politically uninfluential un-

---

[58]This is the special case of unions seeking to preserve (in current union jargon) "relativities" or "established differentials."

fortunates who *cannot* protect themselves from inflation, above the interests of the politically influential who *can,* by continued wage-push. That is ultimately why inflation appears so often to be a government's only way out.[59]

*There is no "profit-push" corresponding to "wage-push"*

The objection may be made that to put the whole blame on organized labor for "the impoverishment factor" is unjust and partisan. Collusive pricing and output fixing are possible, of course, in other sectors of the economy, and all monopolistic exploitation is impoverishing and depressive. But in Britain and most industrialized countries legislative restraints have been imposed on business practices judged to be contrary to the public interest, although similar practices of unionized labor are largely immune. Whether or not for this reason, there seems to be little to parallel the chronic and persistent pressures of wage-push exerted by the trade unions. As Professor Gottfried Haberler has recently insisted,[60] there is no "profit-push" corresponding to "wage-push."

What tends to obscure the situation somewhat is that the market prices of factor inputs and product outputs in general are bid up when aggregate money-spending power increases more rapidly than aggregate purchasing power. But no vicious spiral is activated by this process. Nor need the spiral be set going, with its destructive consequences, when real labor-input and product-output values in a given industry are forced too high to clear markets; for this simply means that market-clearing prices in some noncompeting activities will have to fall. Official policies *could* allow social (i.e., market) pressures of idle (or idling) men and assets in other sectors of the economy to minimize the constriction in the flow of wages and income (by forcing costs down so that they fully clear potential outputs). But when, following one inflationary reduction of real wage rates, strike-threat coercion is allowed once again to discoordinate the economy by restoring or further raising real labor costs, cumulative impoverishment is set going, and seems to be asking for cumulative inflation.

[59]*Politically Impossible. . . ?*, IEA, 1971.
[60]In *Economic Growth and Stability* (Los Angeles: Nash, 1974), p. 113.

Finally, the tendency for inflation to raise residual claims not fixed by contract, such as profits, does not imply that the profits incentive is to blame. The rise in prospective profits reflects the very purpose of inflationary coordination. Monetary authorities seeking fuller employment of men and assets expect that a prospective lag of costs in relation to output prices will make larger investment in labor and plant profitable and so increase the ratios of prices to costs by inflation. Unanticipated inflation thus expands the outputs at which marginal prospective yields are equated with the rate of interest. Unfortunately, observers tend to blame the cure—rising profits—for the disease.[61]

*Inflation prevents us from seeing that depression is due to defects of pricing, not of "demand" or "monetary policy"*

The impression is often left that, in the circumstances discussed, there are no market pressures to restore the flow of wages. That is not so. In a recession incentives do emerge to reduce "excessive" input and output prices (including wage rates) to current market-clearing levels.[62] The basic obstacle is that the unions, and governments acting as though they were agents of the unions, have stood in the way of the restoration of the wages-flow. Had it not been for inflation the community would gradually have learned, from avoidable but bitter experience, that depression is due to the chronic, continuous boosting of costs in occupations and industries where the unions tend to be strongest—because demands for their outputs happen to be most inelastic[63] and consumers therefore most easily exploited. In the absence of inflation it would have been perceived how the withdrawal of labor and output by overpricing in such activities[64] reduces the source of demands for the outputs of less easily exploitable occupations and in-

[61]Below, pp. 114–15.

[62]But market-clearing values are always adjusted to entrepreneurial predictions which, in depression, are justifiably pessimistic (cf. *A Rehabilitation of Say's Law,* pp. 93–102).

[63]That is, demands will not fall off greatly when input costs, and hence profitable output prices, are raised.

[64]A withdrawal of supply occurs whenever the costs of inputs or prices of outputs are raised above the market-clearing level.

dustries. Inflation therefore gravely hinders any general recognition of this reality. And, because the market determination of wage rates has never been tried in the highly unionized industries (and countries), nearly everyone has come to believe that the only way to secure "just" remuneration against avaricious "employers," or against inflation, is through strikes or threats to strike.

*Unanticipated inflation can improve price-cost ratios in many sectors of the economy, but it attracts resources into kinds of production which cannot survive its cessation*

What would happen if, in depression, government did not frustrate the wages restoration process, or allow its private frustration by trade unions, but on the contrary encouraged it? The immediate consequence of cost reductions in any industry would be, as we have seen, to increase the profitability of investment in capital and labor in that industry. But the *major* consequence would be indirect. Each repricing of labor, etc., for market clearance (which, ceteris paribus, would increase the supply of the corresponding output) would express an additional demand for whatever goods or services elsewhere in the economy the receivers of the additional income were destined to acquire. Through favorable reactions upon the ratios of costs to prices, inflation *can* extend the margins at which labor's inputs and replacements of or additions to the stock of assets (materials and equipment) are prospectively profitable (in other words, so that productive activities that would not otherwise be profitable can continue to be so).

But the crudeness of this remedy creates such basic distortions in the pricing mechanism that *we must often blame the attempt to spend depression into prosperity for aggravating prospective and realized unemployment.*[65] For the process leads to men finding kinds of occupation that will no longer remain profitable when the inflation slows down or ceases. Inflation-

[65]This point is more effectively made in F. A. Hayek's addendum to the symposium, *Inflation: Causes, Consequences, Cures,* ed. A. Seldon, IEA Readings 14, 1974. Hayek's title is "Inflation: The Path to Unemployment." It is further discussed by Hayek in *Full Employment At Any Price?,* Occasional Paper 45, IEA, 1975.

induced investments, unless they happen to be in highly versatile assets, will turn out to have been wasteful as soon as inflation ceases to subsidize demand for their product. But workers and physical resources will then have become attached to kinds of economic activity which can no longer cover costs unless further inflation validates the raising of output prices. As Hayek has put it:

> Inflation...gives the whole structure of the economy a distorted, lopsided character which sooner or later makes a more extensive unemployment inevitable than that which that policy was intended to prevent. It does so by drawing more and more workers into kinds of jobs which depend on continuing or even accelerating inflation. And then...every attempt to slow down inflation will at once lead to so much unemployment that the authorities will rapidly abandon it and resume inflation.... We have in fact been led into a frightful position. All politicians promise that they will stop inflation and preserve full employment. But they cannot do this.[66]

In this last sentence, Hayek is assuming that governments are not prepared to repeal minimum wage enactments or to take a stand against unions responsible for the repression of the flow of wages and income through strike-threat pressures. This may not always be so. In Britain a Labour government in 1969 and a Conservative government in 1971 tried to contain the coercive power of the trade unions. It is true that both attempts were repulsed, but it cannot be assumed that, if the economic consequences of the unions' power to disrupt were more clearly understood, such attempts could never succeed. There must be something in the British situation that makes its unions a more stubborn obstruction than unions in Europe appear to be.

### Inflation inevitably comes to be expected

Moreover, although inflation may initially be unanticipated (or not fully anticipated) and hence have some coordinative power when it is first adopted, in due course it inevitably comes to be expected. As soon as the public is tending correctly to predict the planned speed and duration of inflation, and thereby neutralizing its crude coordinative power, the monetary authorities deem it necessary to prevent labor (or

[66]F. A. Hayek, in *Inflation: Causes,* p. 116.

other) input costs from rising ahead of output prices. This they do through a kind of opinion control.

The technique of purposeful inflation does indeed require the "fooling of all the people all the time" about monetary intentions.[67] But all the people cannot be fooled.[68] That is why eventually the crude coordinative consequences become progressively weaker. The result is that the attempt by government or a central bank to slow down inflation or bring it to an end will seem to threaten a serious decline in activity. Even a failure on its part to *accelerate* inflation at the expected pace may bring the prospect of growing joblessness. For such reasons, continued inflation can (in spite of periodic decelerations of the speed of inflation, which seem essential for continuous "fooling the people") seldom fail to engender a wage-push spiral, with additional doses of inflation serving as a habit-forming antidote of diminishing effectiveness to "wage-push."

### Inflation penalizes the innocent with the guilty

The *injustices* of inflation as a remedy for recession have been discussed (pp. 108–10). Because depression is due to input prices, especially labor costs, in key sectors of the economy having been fixed above market-clearing values, remedies which gave high priority to equity would differentiate between people responsible and those not responsible. The inflationary method of restoring prosperity, since Keynes's teaching in the 1930s, operates initially by leaving *money* wage rates and other input prices undisturbed, while reducing *real* wage rates and

---

[67] A fuller discussion and analysis of this proposition is in Milton Friedman, *Unemployment versus Inflation?*, Occasional Paper 44, IEA, 1975, where Professor David Laidler also goes more fully into the developing expectations as studied at the University of Manchester.

[68] Professor James Tobin, who has steadfastly defended reliance on the inflationary (Keynesian) path to prosperity, criticizes economists for what he regards as their "unverified assumption" on this point. He holds it *is* possible to "fool all the people all the time." *(New York Review of Books,* May 6, 1971.) See Haberler's cogent criticism of Tobin *(Economic Growth,* p. 94). Haberler points out that, a year later, in his presidential address to the American Economic Association, Tobin did not repeat this suggestion, although he continued to argue that permanent inflation could be beneficial and harmless even when fully anticipated. Tobin set this thesis in an impressive display of modern economic techniques. But I hold his assumptions to be quite unacceptable.

the *real* values of priced inputs generally. But this includes labor costs which are *not* above market-clearing values as well as those which *are*. That is, the impact of currency debasement is to reduce not only the purchasing power of money incomes which have been raised through strike-threat coercion (and hence have been causing the depression), but also the incomes of persons whose remuneration has been determined solely in the free market, without duress. Inflation, which remains the favored remedy of the Keynesians, though Keynes might not have argued for it in 1975, hits the guilty and the innocent in the same manner and degree.[69]

## Wage and price controls also penalize the innocent with the guilty

An even cruder remedy, resorted to when inflation begins to scare too many people, is what is called euphemistically an "incomes policy." In practice, what is meant is various forms of wage and price controls. Like inflation, the controls penalize the innocent along with the guilty. Often, indeed, they discriminate in favor of the guilty parties because union members possess the strongest political influence. Even in the absence of such discrimination, the controls freeze competitively determined prices and incomes as well as those resulting from coercion or monopolistic collusion. Worst of all, although "there is no 'profit push' corresponding to 'wage-push,' " in order to create an appearance of justice the controls are aimed at residual claims (i.e., profits) which, in a depression of the "stagflation" type, will already have been squeezed through strike-threat concessions, as a quid pro quo for freezing wage rates. Unfortunately, there is no more effective way of curtailing or wiping out demands for labor than restraint of profits. For it is rising prospective profits—rising prospective yields to investment in labor's (and other) inputs—which lead

---

[69] A once-and-for-all bout of inflation (in spite of its clumsy nature and its unjust incidence) would be capable of temporarily restoring "full employment" (although not "optimal employment"), while the newly established set of prices could then survive without the prospect of further inflation and without the reemergence of depression. But for that to happen, the private use of coercive power would have to be forbidden.

to increased employment with higher wage rates yet a higher wages flow (pp. 110–11).

## Remedies for Chronic Strike-Threat Impoverishment

### *The case against strikes would hold even if the legal immunities of unions were withdrawn*

The argument has suggested the indefensibility, in a civilized community, of what has been called "the peaceful strike." The disruption of the market system by the simple, concerted withdrawal of labor is in itself damaging to the community. Unfortunately, political acquiescence in the strike weapon has enabled other forms of coercive power to be used to supplement it.

In the course of a "dispute," unions have acquired legal immunities from civil prosecution and from indictment for what would be criminal acts if perpetrated by others. Rioting, intimidation, physical violence—assaults on nonstrikers, strikebreakers and others—have continued to be a frequent accompaniment of recent strikes in the Western world generally.[70] It is hardly surprising that, in a community which refrains from police action against such practices, as in Britain in 1972, the right to strike "peacefully" is acquiesced in.

But the argument would stand even if the civil and criminal immunities of the unions were abolished. Some people believe that, if the prospects of physical violence could be eliminated from the strike threat, and antimonopoly law (antitrust) were applied to labor without discrimination, the trade union organization, otherwise more or less in its existing form, could usefully survive. Such an experiment might be revealing, but the truth is that it was the power wielded by union hierarchies in Western countries through the right to strike "peacefully" that enabled them to win such immunities for their organizations. It may be useful, therefore, to consider briefly how the union organization would be affected if the right to coerce were ruled out.

---

[70]Adam Smith remarked that striking workmen's combinations always have "recourse to the loudest clamour, and sometimes to the most shocking violence and outrages". *(Wealth of Nations,* 1776, Cannan edition, p. 67.)

## Reform prospects: "collective bargaining" without strikes

All fundamental changes in human institutions which have come about without bloodshed have retained old forms while new realities have emerged. The initial step towards reform could permit the retention of existing union organizations and their officials. "Collective bargaining" would, however, presumably come to mean that union managements would begin to act entrepreneurially on their members' behalf, finding better paid employment for "underpaid" members, or jobs with better prospects. Any worker may be held to be "underpaid" if his earnings are less than he could command elsewhere if he were better informed. Unions would have the expert task of taking the initiative in these circumstances. Moreover, in the event of an alleged general underpayment of workers by a firm, the union would have the function of warning the management of an imminent gradual outflow of personnel (not to threaten a collusive and simultaneous withdrawal) to superior jobs.

The intention of such a policy would be to force the firm to compete effectively with alternative employment outlets. And the unions would retain the right and duty to ensure the effectiveness of their members' legal rights (such as the enforcement of wage contracts not accepted by managements under duress, or suing for damages in the event of alleged managerial misrepresentation.)[71]

## Predictable consequences of a strike-free era

Ideally, what is needed for the emancipation of labor is the enactment of the principle underlying the British Combination Acts of 1799 and 1800 (pp. 18–19, 69–70) adapted to the 1970s. Almost unbelievable falsification on the part of the Hammonds and other "historians" (p. 118) has left the impression that these acts were harshly enforced. The truth is the reverse.[72]

---

[71]Cf. *The Strike-Threat System,* pp. 111–12.

[72]M. D. George, "The Combination Laws Reconsidered," *Economic Journal Supplement,* 1927; J. A. Lincoln, *Journey to Coercion,* IEA, 1964, pp. 17–21. The Tolpuddle ringleaders were treated with surprising leniency for an age in which severe penalties for small crimes was normal. But they were not "martyrs." And they were not charged under the Combination Acts. Their offense was under the Unlawful Oaths Offences Act of 1797. Moreover, they were ex-

The acts consolidated ancient common law against "conspiracy," and some forty anticonspiracy statutes applying to particular industries; they were intended to protect the people from exploitation as consumers. Their important principle is that they forbad action to fix prices in concert ("conspiracy" or "combination") among suppliers of goods and services. They were, however, never effectively enforced and were repealed (by subterfuge) in 1824. The relevant point is that under these acts strikes were illegal. If an up-to-date version were reenacted in Britain today making attempts at concerted withdrawal of labor illegal, the beneficial consequences for the workers could, I maintain, be enormous. In the British inflationary recession of 1975, for instance, the reform could bring forth recovery as sensational and rapid as Professor Erhard's "German Miracle" inaugurated in 1949. We could expect it to cause an almost unprecedented increase in an uninflated wages and income flow.[73]

The strike-threat obstacle to prosperity without inflation can now be discussed. But we must first emphasize that the reform suggested:
  (i) would bring to an end an era of distributive injustices and tolerated poverty-creation;
  (ii) would raise the material welfare of perhaps 90 percent of the people;
  (iii) would release resources for new occupations in which the product enriches life;
  (iv) would enormously improve employment security; and, above all,
  (v) would bring about an unprecedented improvement in the quality of human relations.

Because of the difficulty of conveying these truths, perhaps the most promising approach to reform would be to capitalize on the growing alarm at the curse of inflation, and work for a five-year moratorium from strikes and union violence, accompanied by a specific commitment to a *complete* cessation of in-

---

plicitly warned of the penalties under the act by the justices, who tried their utmost to avoid a prosecution. (*The Strike-Threat System,* pp. 29–38; D. Dewey, *Monopoly in Economics and the Law* (Chicago: Rand McNally, 1959), p. 117. [73]*A Rehabilitation of Say's Law,* chapters 12 and 18.

flation.[74] If such a reform were so steadfastly enforced that entrepreneurs really trusted that it would not be sabotaged and that privately organized coercion and intimidation were ruled out, entrepreneurial optimism would lead to an immediate increase in the demand for labor.

### The myth of "labor's long and bitter struggle"

Before the argument for so basic a reform can be effectively communicated, it may be imperative to win recognition for the truth that:

1. *since the beginning of the industrial era* the unions, relying on the power to strike, have been seeking their members' private advantage by methods which have harmed others;
2. in so doing they have been depressing the wages flow (and hence the average wage rate);
3. they have been rendering income distribution far less equal than the free market would have determined;
4. they have been creating avoidable poverty; and
5. in the present age they have been mainly responsible for the political expediency of inflation (p. 116).

It may be that attempts to convey these truths will fail unless the widely taught notions or myths about "labor's long and bitter struggle" for economic justice are first dispelled. The more hardy legends about the nineteenth-century oppression and deprivation of the workers before they were organized in trade unions to win "equality of bargaining power" have been tenacious.[75]

---

[74]That is, a commitment to maintain a long-term price index constant, in the sense that the larger any deviation from the zero trend of the index (to which the monetary authority would be committed), the stronger would be the pressure for the direction of the deviation to be reversed.

[75]*The Strike-Threat System,* chap. 3. On the correction of British history the reader is referred to F. A. Hayek, ed., *Capitalism and the Historians,* Chicago University Press, 1954, and A. Seldon, ed., *The Long Debate on Poverty.* There is still resistance to the evidence of historical researches in the last few decades that suggest a different interpretation from that of the Hammonds and the Webbs. School and "popular" histories in Britain are still influenced by the older view that industrialization depressed rather than raised general living standards.

## *Compulsory arbitration is no remedy*

Compulsory arbitration has been thought to be a means of curbing strike-threat abuses. It might possibly ameliorate the worst consequences, but it implies acceptance of the present system: arbitration, voluntary or mandatory, presupposes a strike or a threat to strike. It thus seems to regard the determination of the value of labor's inputs through a kind of "warfare" as basically defensible, one party or the other being simply presumed to be holding out for unreasonable surrender terms.

But the real opposing parties in an industrial dispute are not the union members, on the one side, and the investors against whom the strike threat is directed, on the other. The main opposite party to the union members consists of the people whose incomes are gained in noncompeting activities, because it is the demands for their inputs or outputs that are restricted. In the absence of joint monopoly[76] the interests of stockholders, as well as of consumers, are that strike-threat demands be resisted. But in resisting union coercion, managements are defending the whole community as investors and as consumers, and not only the owners of the assets employed in their industry or firm. In these circumstances, an arbitrator can act in accordance with principle only if he accepts his role as that of protecting the public from exploitation; and then he is acting more in what Americans call an "antitrust" capacity than as an arbitrator. But in such a role he would have to recognize that the interests of labor *as a whole* and the interests of the public coincide. For the reduction of such wage rates as have been imposed under the strike threat, or under other kinds of coercion, raises the flow of real wages, causes more equality and security of income, and benefits the community in its role as consumer.

Defensible arbitration must be founded on a recognition that:

> Within any area sheltered by economic distance, by human inertias and by union-imposed restraints, in the absence of any "shut-in" of labor contrived on behalf of investors, the flow of wages will be highest and the distribution of the flow will be most

[76]Above, pp. 67–72, 83–84, 99–100.

equitable, when every wage rate is fixed at the lowest level
necessary to retain or attract labor for each activity judged to be
profitable.[77]

The good sense of this proposition is generally recognized
when it applies to buying raw materials where they are
cheapest. But an employee's input—his contribution to "work
in progress"—is also a product. The determination of its value
by the social forces of the market is equally in the general interest, whereas the determination of its value by private forces
(e.g., by government edict in reaction to private interest
groups, or by union coercion) must (almost) always be contrary
to the general good.

### The limited power of government, and the power of the market

"What the public must learn...," writes Hayek, is that "it
is simply no longer in the power of government to maintain full
employment and a tolerable productive organisation of the
economy."[78] The public must also learn that what governments
cannot do, the market can.

To quote Hayek further, it will

take great courage—and almost more understanding than one
dares to hope for—on the part of the government to make the
people understand what the position is. We are probably ap-
proaching a critical test of democracy about the outcome of
which we must feel apprehensive.[79]

But so formidable would be the task of communicating to influential opinion makers on this point that, if the chronic impoverishment is to be early reversed, the best tactics will probably be to concentrate on the more obvious evidence of current
burdens. It ought to be possible to establish, beyond genuine
doubt, what we have tried to demonstrate here, namely, that
*the expediency of inflation has throughout been due to the
widespread overruling of market-clearing wage rates, prices,
and values by private coercion and government edict.*

[77]*The Strike-Threat System,* p. 103.
[78]Hayek, in *Inflation,* ed. Seldon, p. 120.
[79]Hayek, ibid., p. 120.

This is precisely the situation in Britain and other parts of the English-speaking world as the new part 3 of the second edition of this book is prepared for publication, forty-five years after the first edition.

## Collective Bargaining without Strikes

There is no implication that, if deprived of the right to strike, the trade unions would be left with no socially useful task in collective bargaining and other activities. In some of their functions they form essential machinery in a free-market economy. Thus they *could* act entrepreneurially on behalf of their members, thereby assisting the process of maximizing the wages flow instead of repressing it.

### Strike-threat impoverishment

But we have shown that, relying on strike power, the unions have, from the beginning of the industrial age, operated as a regressive and impoverishing influence. Before the First World War, the impoverishment, although burdensome, was relatively minor. But during the last decade, the intensification of collective bargaining under the strike threat, which has throughout countervailed in some measure the benign consequences of thrift and entrepreneurial acumen upon the wages-flow, has often more than countervailed it. By the continued private use of coercive power, technological and managerial potentialities which could have vastly improved the material welfare of the people, as well as the quality of life in their moral *and* nonmaterial well-being, have been frustrated. The threat to disrupt the entrepreneurial process by the concerted withdrawal of labor (boosted by supplementary force) has:

1. severely curtailed the wages-flow;
2. raised the cost of the capital resources which constitute labor's tools;
3. caused the assets stock to assume a composition that is relatively invulnerable to capital confiscation through the threat to strike;
4. extensively attenuated the wage-multiplying power of the assets provided;

5. aggravated inequalities of income;
6. materially worsened industrial relations, tending to destroy the workers' dignity, their pride in achievement and sense of purpose;
7. often frustrated attempts to improve conditions of employment in the workshop and office;
8. militated against the market provision of employment security; and
9. through the increasing pressures of "wage-push" in recent years, been mainly responsible for the political expediency of inflation.

## The burden

If political democracy and economic freedom survive in Britain and the United States, future economic historians will come to regard public acquiescence in the burden of unnecessarily low incomes and distributive injustices as almost incredible. The truth is that strike-threat force has contributed to the reduction of Britain to the status of a second-rate economic and political power. It has hamstrung the formidable potential productive capacity of the United States and thereby weakened her ability to contribute to the maintenance of world peace. Almost the only beneficiaries of the system have been the union hierarchies and politicians for whom the existence of poverty provides a profitable situation.

The kind of "antipoverty program" resorted to is that of income transfers in various forms. Such transfers do of course mitigate the burden *temporarily;* but the result is to obscure the origins of the basic impoverishment and hence to perpetuate it. In every case the ultimate burden is aggravated, and with regressive incidence. Income transfers from the provident and the industrious to the improvident and the indolent have been squandering the people's capital, as Evan Durbin, a leading British Labour economist, courageously admitted in 1940.[80] Humanitarians who believe that to strike is a basic human right, used to further economic justice, have been misled.

[80]E. F. M. Durbin, *The Politics of Democratic Socialism* (London: Routledge, 1940).

# Envoi: Observations
on the General Argument

Observations on the General Argument

*LORD FEATHER*

*Assistant Secretary, Trades Union Congress, 1947–60*
*Assistant General Secretary, Trades Union Congress, 1960–69*
*General Secretary, Trades Union Congress, 1969–73*
*President, European Trade Union Confederation, 1973–74*

As a trade unionist it is difficult for me to review Professor Hutt's book, and particularly part 3, without bias. But I feel excused to a considerable degree by the prejudice of Professor Hutt himself. He seems so dedicated to the principle of the free market that he excludes almost any kind of qualification there may be to blunt the effects of a free-market economy; but, at the same time, he advances ideas to limit the rights of unions to operate freely.

When Professor Hutt, whose book is both stimulating and, to me, irritating, says that the redistribution of income from rich to poor is universally claimed as the chief *raison d'être* for trade unionism, he is paying more attention to the esoteric arguments of some economists than he is to trade union thought.

From practical experience I know that this is not so.

The reason for collective bargaining in the minds of the millions of trade unionists is for the purpose of maintaining and improving the living standards of their members. Fortunately, that takes trade unionists into a field of consideration not only of the amount of wages in the pay packet, but the amount of wages in relation to prices in general. They are concerned therefore with purchasing power in an existing economy and the present-day society. But living standard involves also a consideration of the economy in general. For workpeople to have a wage rate which may be satisfactory in relation to the price level is one thing, but it is no use having a satisfactory nominal wage level unless there is the opportunity of earning those wages, and that takes them into questions of full employment, international relationships, imports and exports, world prices, the balance of trade, and the balance of payments.

Professor Hutt makes me shudder when he says that over the last 100–150 years the trade union movement has failed to improve the living standards of its members. What he says is that without trade union action and representation the living standard would in fact be what it is now, or better. He may believe that, but ten million trade unionists in the TUC would not. Education, health, safety, social standards generally—better if trade unions had not existed? One almost thinks that Professor Hutt is so fascinated with industrial archaeology that the economics and social policies of a modern society are out of sight. In case this is thought to be a distortion of his case, look at what he says:

> Ideally, what is needed for the emancipation of labor is the enactment of the principle underlying the British Combination Acts of 1799 and 1800 adapted to the 1970s.... The relevant point is that under these acts strikes were illegal. (pp. 117–18)

If the strike threat has been responsible, as Professor Hutt says, for limiting the growth of the economy and has resulted in impediments to improvements of workers' living standards, one must look around to see if there is a society in which the strike threat does not obtain and consider the relative living standards of human beings. The strike threat does not obtain in Russia. It did not exist in Nazi Germany or in Mussolini's Italy. If it were true that the nonexistence of strike threat in itself meant automatic improvement in living standards, then Professor Hutt would need to point to living standards in totalitarian states as being an improvement on the living standards in Britain, Western Europe generally, and the United States. Now, who would believe that?

Professor Hutt's thesis adduces arguments which could never be based on a full understanding of an industrial society such as that which exists in Britain.

A good deal of detail in Professor Hutt's book is worthy of reflection and discussion by industrialists and trade unionists; but its main theme seems so extravagantly biased against modern trade unionism that it is doubtful whether it will be given the objective examination which it ought to have.

And that's a pity.

## SIR LEONARD NEAL

*Labor Relations Adviser, Esso Europe Inc.*
*Member of the British Railways Board, 1967-74*
*Visiting Professor of Industrial Relations, Institute of Science and Technology, University of Manchester, since 1970*
*Chairman, Commission on Industrial Relations, 1971-74*

The world of politics and economics, from time to time, needs someone like W. H. Hutt who cares to think about the unthinkable and to question the accepted conventions of current thought. Until twenty years ago it was possible to set examination questions in economic theory—at least half seriously—that asked undergraduates to "discuss the claim that trade unions are not capable of affecting the allocation of resources or the redistribution of wealth by the system of collective bargaining." The implications, of course, were always to test the student's understanding of perfect competition, of marginal utility, of other theories of wage determination and the restrictions these theories placed on the effectiveness of trade union action over the long term.

I use the term "half-seriously" deliberately because until twenty years ago the impact of trade union activity, particularly throughout Western economies, could hardly be ignored. The superficial, short-term evidence of the redistributive effects of collective bargaining seemed irrefutable—particularly to the trade unions themselves and the "new economists" amongst the labor correspondents of the mass media.

What tended to be overlooked (in general terms) was that the main factors in the redistribution of wealth and income were political and social rather than purely economic: the product of progressive penal taxation and "welfare" policies. Further, the conclusions relied on short-term empirical evidence much more than long-term trends. If a real redistribution had not taken place, how else could we account for the new affluence of the mass of blue-collar workers with all the appurtenances of wealth—of freezers, cars, color television, foreign holidays, etc? If the "new poor" were remembered at all, they were still thought of as the helpless victims of capitalism rather than of unfettered, free collective bargaining. If any further doubts existed they were overwhelmed by the demands of the apologists of collective bargaining for "no interference in free collective bargaining," "no unemployment," "higher pensions," "more homes," "more investment," "lower prices," and the final, clinching argument—"lower profits." The contradictions in all these competing claims produced little comment even when they were further negated by the latest and most extravagant wage claims that were bound to defeat all the purposes involved.

The explanation of this phenomenon is to be found only in the ingenuous acceptance of a number of widely held shibboleths—that the

> operation of the market is inherently unfair and that trade union action made it fairer; that trade unions by their actions secured a redistribution from rich to poor and thus that such action was not only just but egalitarian; and because of this the trade unions were the *true* reformers who alone were concerned with poverty and unfairness.

It is, of course, true that a few voices are raised from time to time to question the existence of the new "emperor's new clothes"; to point to the violence done to the argument by the increasing strikes, picketing, restrictionism, and the paradox of higher wages, employment, investment, and social benefits concurrently with claims for lower prices and lower profits. But such voices were and are overwhelmed because the trade unions, in many Western democracies, have not merely captured the attention of the mass media but also the thinking and policies of political parties. Thus we have politicians of all shades competing for the attention and support of trade unions by pursuing programs that are not merely irrelevant, not merely unsupported by the majority, but are positively harmful in the long run. What is perhaps not being noticed, however, is that the "long run" is becoming shorter and shorter.

So, while one has some reservations about a few of Professor Hutt's arguments and conclusions, he is nevertheless owed a great debt for the refreshing coolness of his analysis and theory. For he has pointed our attention not merely to the consequences of collective bargaining—which many of us had thought were merely due to the excesses of the system—but to the fallacies in the basic premise on which the system rests. And he has exposed the sophistries of the premise with irresistible logic and merciless clarity.

## PROFESSOR HUTT

Shortly after the galley proofs of part 3 had been passed, three articles of great contemporary relevance entitled "Unions Within the Law" were published.[1] The authors are statesmen of eminence in all three British political parties: Lords Byers and George-Brown, and Mr. Edward Heath. Hence it seems appropriate in this "envoi" to comment on their contributions.

None of the three touches on what I have here treated as the fundamental question, namely, are the unions fulfilling their chief claimed purpose? Are they *really* bringing about a transfer of income from "capital" to "labor"? I have been concerned almost entirely with the answer to this question and its implications. The three articles expose grave uneasiness in the highest quarters in Britain about strike power.

### Abuse of power

The authors differ considerably on some points, but all three have this in common: They are deeply perturbed because they feel that the unions, in wielding a power that they (the authors) accept as defensible in principle, have abused it. The abuse alleged is that use of the threat to strike is now going too far. In contrast, I have tried to prove that, in a free society, strike power is indefensible *in and of itself.*

[1] *Daily Telegraph,* August 27–29, 1975.

Lord George-Brown, a member of the British Labour Party with a trade union background, blames union excesses chiefly on the infiltration of the unions by what he calls "the Communists," and he points out that the unions are not alone in this respect.

The most important concrete recommendation in Lord George-Brown's prescient and courageous article is the abandonment of "mass-meeting" decisions by the unions on important issues. For at such meetings, he says, "attendance is not representative...the opportunities for intimidation are limitless and no one can count the hands." He suggests further the adoption of "a compulsory secret and preferably postal ballot...[with] independent counting." And he claims that his "fellow trade unionists would not merely acquiesce in but positively applaud" such reforms. "The leaders might fulminate."

Lord George-Brown refers to the failure of political leadership in Britain. He condemns sheer lack of moral courage, "the desire not to fall out with anyone," and policies designed for "mere survival in office." These weaknesses have brought Britain to her present impasse. A "debilitated Parliament," he says, and the pusillanimity and spinelessness of the executive are allowing power to pass "from the shaking nerveless hands at the centre to stronger and power-hungry hands elsewhere."

### "Submission" to union power?

Mr. Edward Heath (the former Conservative British prime minister) appears at times to illustrate this very point. He is clearly aware of the ominous usurpation of government authority by the unions; but he urges acquiescence in this usurpation because it is now "the reality of industrial life." It means, he says, "accepting that trade unions have greater power," and giving the unions "new responsibility to match that power." Does not the word "accepting" here simply mean "submitting to"?

All three recognize that the growing union power is being used irresponsibly. Why, then, does not one of them recommend legislative prohibition of the irresponsible acts they have in mind? Only the Labour Lord George-Brown shows real understanding of the issue. Yet even he suggests that "there is no way in which the law should or could be used to limit or control what is called 'union power.' ''

Mr. Heath acknowledges that inflation—which results from governments' efforts to mitigate the impoverishing consequences of wage-push—has been "disastrous." But, he says rather weakly, government and managements can also be blamed. This common half-truth suggests that all parties are *equally* guilty. It ought never to be stated without the most candid admission that "there is no 'profit push' corresponding to 'wage push,' '' as Professor Gottfried Haberler has recently insisted in a work of the greatest importance. Haberler points out, in various contexts, that

> the power of business monopolies and union monopolies...is quantitatively though not qualitatively very different.... The impact of business monopolies on inflation is small compared with that of unions.... The equation of business monopolies and labour monopolies...completely misjudges the comparative strength of the two.[2]

Of course, blame does attach to government but only because of official inaction (apart from inflation) in the face of wage-push impoverishment and the demoralization of managements for this reason.

## Impoverishing effects

Even if the abuses to which I have briefly referred on page 116 were abandoned, and the indefensible practices Lord George-Brown exposes so clearly were eliminated by law, my basic argument would remain valid. He perceives that the unions are not having the effects their defenders have been led to believe, although he is hardly specific. But I have shown that the effects are diametrically opposite to what the general public supposes. The pressures which the British unions have exerted since the repeal of the Combination Acts in 1824 have been continuously constraining (but fortunately not wholly suppressing) those increases in the aggregate wages-flow brought about by thrift, entrepreneurial risk taking, and economizing inventiveness.

[2]Gottfried Haberler, *Economic Growth and Stability* (Los Angeles: Nash, 1974) chapters 6 and 7.

If my diagnosis is valid, the poor have throughout been harmed more than in proportion to their poverty. Indeed, even before trade union activities in Britain began to be dictated by minorities, all the arguments I have submitted were relevant. The consequence in Britain has been, not to initiate, but merely *to aggravate,* the impoverishment process which, I have tried to show, is the inevitable outcome of strike-threat power.

### *"Beggar-my-neighbor" attitudes*

Lord Byers of the Liberal Party also emphasizes the formidable and still growing power that the unions have acquired through their ability to coerce governments (as well as managements operating in the market). "One major union," he says, "can bring a country to a halt." Policies which are "not...representative of the desires of the broad mass of the electorate" have, he asserts, been forced upon the present government. He mentions the "need for debate," warning that the "whole question of 'industrial democracy' has not been thought through." He tells the unions in this context that

> it is a total misuse of the term "democracy" to exclude from participation [in, say, works councils] all those who fail to join a union....

He warns them that their policy is amounting to one of "beggar my neighbor to beggar myself." And most important of all, he perceives that, when a powerful union seizes

> a bigger slice of the national cake than its contribution warrants...it is the poor, the pensioners, and the low-paid who are the first to suffer.

Lord Byers does not perceive, however, that capitulation to strike power virtually always, almost without exception, has this effect. The regressive and impoverishing consequence of forcing up labor costs is not a recent experience. It has been a universal phenomenon. Nor does he recognize my argument[3] that "the slice" that the workers' contribution "warrants" is that determined in a truly free market.

---

[3]Especially in part 3, chap. 3.

Thus although the symptoms that disturb Lord George-Brown, Lord Byers and Mr. Heath are highly important, they merely reflect the underlying conditions I have analyzed in this book. It is not sufficient to refer to indefensible practices that all can recognize. It is necessary, as I have tried to do, to go much deeper to the still misunderstood causes, attitudes, and solutions.

# ABOUT THE AUTHOR

W. H. Hutt was born in London in 1899. He trained as a pilot in the RFC and the RAF during World War One and afterwards attended the London School of Economics, earning a bachelor's degree in commerce. In 1928 he joined the faculty of the University of Cape Town, South Africa, and was appointed professor and dean in 1931 of the faculty of commerce there. Later he served as director of the university's Graduate School of Business.

The author has received many appointments as visiting professor to universities in the United States: at the University of Virginia, Rockford College, Stanford University, Wabash College, California State College, and the University of Dallas.

Among the books by Professor Hutt are *Economics and the Public* (1936); *The Theory of Idle Resources* (1939); *Keynesianism — Retrospect and Prospect* (1936); *The Economics of the Colour Bar* (1964); *Politically Impossible...?* (1971); *The Strike-Threat System* (1973); and *A Rehabilitation of Say's Law* (1974).

# The Cato Papers

Reprinted by the Cato Institute, the Papers in this series have been selected for their singular contributions to such fields as economics, history, philosophy, and public policy.

Copies of the *Cato Papers* may be ordered from the Publications Department, Cato Institute, 747 Front Street, San Francisco, California 94111.